Barb:

I was Thinking about
you, so I sent you
my new book. If The
ever a True worshiper it
Thankyou for your example, love a
support!

Love,
Rick Rannie

True Worship

RICK RANNIE

Scripture taken from the King James Version of the Bible.

This book is a work of non-fiction. Unless otherwise noted, the author and the publisher make no explicit guarantees as to the accuracy of the information contained in this book and in some cases, names of people and places have been altered to protect their privacy.

WestBow Press books may be ordered through booksellers or by contacting:

WestBow Press
A Division of Thomas Nelson & Zondervan
1663 Liberty Drive
Bloomington, IN 47403
www.westbowpress.com
1 (866) 928-1240

ISBN: 978-1-5127-0992-6 (sc)
ISBN: 978-1-5127-0993-3 (hc)
ISBN: 978-1-5127-0991-9 (e)

Library of Congress Control Number: 2015913761

Print information available on the last page.

WestBow Press rev. date: 8/31/2015

Contents

Preface

I have always found the Scripture in John 4:23 that talks about how the Father searches for true worshipers to be fascinating. They are those who worship in Spirit and in truth. Questions abounded in my mind as to how one obtains such a distinction in their life? What does worshipping in Spirit and truth look like?

In my last book, “Beyond the Glory of God,” it dealt with the process of coming into the glory of God. We go from life which is receiving the Lord, to the glory of God. The glory of God is the presence of God in our lives. It is the essence, light or life that emanates off the person of God. The glory then leads us to the kingdom of God. It is the sign that the kingdom is with us. The kingdom of God is coming into the reality of the Father and Jesus being with you. We will deal with the kingdom of God within this book later. To come into this experience of the glory and the Kingdom of God we must come into an abiding relationship with God. We have an abiding relationship because of the cross of Jesus Christ and it is part of our inheritance. When we know that the Father and Jesus are with us then we know that we are in an abiding relationship with the Lord. It is here that we learn to walk as mature sons and daughters of God. We can walk with God as the men and women of the Bible did.

The glory of God is being in God and Him in us. God once told me to ask that I come to know the full extent of His glory. He takes us from glory to glory. There is a place of knowing the glory in us. Paul calls this the riches of glory (Ephesians 3: 14-21). These riches are: to be strengthened in the inner man, Christ dwelling in your heart by faith, being rooted and grounded in love, to know love, the Father dwelling in you, the power of God in you, and revival. These are some of the results of the glory being in us. What a glorious blessing we have in God by having His glory in us. But God says do not be satisfied. As I stated before, the Lord told me once to ask to come into the full extent of His glory. God wants us to also to experience the outward manifestation or expression of His glory. Some would call this the Shekinah Glory. This term is seen in Exodus 40:35, where the cloud came and made its abode on the tent and Moses could not enter. It is also seen in Isaiah 60:1, where it says, “Arise and shine for your light has come and the glory is risen on you and will be seen on you.” This is what David speaks of in Psalm 139: 5, where he says, “he is beset before and behind by the Lord. The Lord has also laid His hand on him.” This is what is talked about in Psalm 91:1; he that dwells in the secret place of the most High shall abide under the shadow of the Almighty. God is standing right there with us. The outward expression of glory is real. It is realizing that God Himself is with us (Revelation 21:3). This is what Paul was talking about when he said walk in the Spirit. This is the Kingdom of God when the Father and Jesus come and make their abode with you. The Father and Jesus are the kingdom, glory and power.

Once we have the life, glory and the kingdom of God then what? What is our purpose in life? I used to think ministry to people was my purpose. But what happens if the Lord does not have you ministering for a time. The Lord said if I never did another thing He would still love me. His love is not based on what we do. He loves us because we are His beloved children. I have found that our first ministry is to be to the Lord.

The Father and Jesus come to us because of love. 2 Chronicles 7:16 says, “He will give us His eyes and heart perpetually.” The word perpetually means from sunrise to sunset. When the Father and Jesus comes to your house how do you act?

The Word says in (John 4: 23-24):

> *23. But the hour cometh, and now is, when the true worshipers shall worship the Father in spirit and in truth: for the Father seekth such to worship Him.*
>
> *24. God is a Spirit: and they that worship Him must worship Him in spirit and in truth.*

This book will look at what does it mean to be a true worshiper. It is important to be a true worshiper because the Word says that the Father is looking for those who are true worshipers. To worship means to minister to someone. The picture is a dog licking his master's feet. I used to wonder why God needed praise and worship. One day the Lord gave me a vision of what worship does to Him. When we worship Him it is like a wave of joy that overshadows Him. It brings Him joy. Psalm 16:11, says in His presence is fullness of joy and at His right hand pleasures forevermore. When I worship Him the joy and pleasure He feels overshadows us. It was a beautiful picture of the ministry we can bring to the Lord when we are not focused on ourselves. The key to worship is love. Simply said we are to worship because the Lord is just looking for someone to love Him back.

Acknowledgments

I dedicate this book to my dear cousin Dr. Sharon Wattley-Hudson who went home to the Lord way too early. She now knows what true worship looks like in heaven. I also dedicate this book to her husband Michael, daughters Skylar, and Samantha, mother Peggy Wattley, and her brother and sister-in-law Daryn and Ingrid Wattley. I also want to thank Joan Lisle for editing. I bless them with peace, comfort and victory.

Chapter 1

The Heart of God

According as He hath chosen us
in Him before the foundation of the world,
that we should be holy and without blame
before Him in love. Ephesians 1:4

Love is the key to worship. The reason we worship is simply because the Lord is looking for someone to love Him back. Love is the foundation for anyone who desires to be a true worshiper. However the problem arises in our ability to love God as He asks. As we are on this journey, we will find this task to be impossible in and of ourselves. The Word says we love God because He first loved us. So the way to love is through the cross of Jesus. I found that in and of myself I could not love God with my all. I tried to do it. There was much prayer, but I never thought I was pleasing to God.

Jesus said that as we obey we love God. It seemed to me that I was always coming up short. I could say with Paul, "O wretched man that I am who will deliver me from this body of death?" (Romans 7:24). After years of frustration trying to walk this out with the Lord, I came across Ephesians 1:4. According to Ephesians 1:4, God has chosen us in Jesus so that we be holy and before Him in love. We are placed into Jesus, who is love, so that we can be before the Father in love. Jesus is made holiness and love for us in Him. Remember that God is looking for true worshipers. Love is the place of true worship.

In 1 Corinthians 13:1-13, Paul shows that if I move in ministry and do not have love then it is not worth anything. In 1 Corinthians 12, Paul talks about the gifts but in chapter 13 he is showing us a better way and that is love. He says we minister in part or the ministry is not as it should be without love. Paul shows that the problem is solved when that which is perfect is come, which is Jesus. Paul says when he was a child he spoke or worshiped as a child, he understood and thought as a child. But when he became a man he put away childish things. The childish things are the gifts. I am not saying the gifts are not necessary but when we move in the realm of love God uses the anointing on us to do the work. When David was anointed the Spirit of the Lord was with him from that day forward (1 Samuel 16:1). The gifts used in love will cause you to minister on a different level. The gifts are expressions of His power.

Jesus was anointed with the Holy Ghost and power, went about doing good works and healed all those who were oppressed of the devil because God was with Him (Acts 10:38). When you move in love you know the Father and Jesus are with you. This is beyond just moving in the realm of being gifted. When Jesus comes then we know it is Jesus that does the works. Our worship must become a mature worship where we are not doing praise and worship for ourselves but because of love. Our first ministry is to the Father and Jesus. It is then that ministry, refreshing and revival will come to the people. In Exodus there was a distinction made between Moses and the prophets. The Lord said He speaks to the prophets in visions and dreams. We can say the prophets were gifted. However, Moses was not like them because he saw the similitude of the Lord and was face to face with Him. This was a place of intimacy beyond just being gifted.

This is what Paul is talking about in
1 Corinthians 13:12:

For now we see through a glass darkly, but then face to face: now I know in part; but then shall I know even as also I am known.

The place of love God brings us to is the heart or love of God. This is the place we are to dwell in as children of God. In 2 Chronicles 7, God talks about giving His heart to the people. Psalm 91:1, talks about the secret place that is the heart or love of God. Throughout the Bible there are references made about a dwelling place for us to experience in the spirit realm. Below is a list of these:

- The secret place _ Psalm 91:1
- The tabernacle, the holy hill _ Psalm 15:1
- The house of God _ Psalm 23:6
- That I may dwell in the house of the Lord _ Psalm 27:4
- God dwells in the high and holy place _ Isaiah 57:15
- Thy habitation _ Psalm 91:9
- Our dwelling place in all generations _ Psalm 90:1
- High and Holy place _ Isaiah 57:15
- Strong habitation _ Psalm 71:3
- In my Father's house are many mansions: if it were not so, I would have told you. I go to prepare a place for you _ John 14:2

- Made a pillar in the temple of God _ Revelation 3:12
- No temple, for the Lord God Almighty and the Lamb are the temple of it _ Revelation 21:22
- He that dwells in love dwells in God and God in him _ 1 John 4: 15-16

When we look at the above Scriptures we can assume that there is a dwelling place we can experience as Christians. This is not a place we can only experience when we go to heaven when we die, but it is a place we can experience now. It is the place of rest spoken about in Hebrews chapter 3. David prayed that he would dwell in His house all the days of his life (Psalms 27:4).

Psalm 91 talks about dwelling in the secret place of the Most High, and that those that do this will abide under the shadow of the Almighty. There is a Scripture in the Song of Solomon 2: 3-4, that gives insight into Psalm 91.

> *3. As the apple tree among the trees of the wood, so is my beloved among the sons. I sat down under* ***his shadow*** *with great delight, and his fruit was sweet to my taste.*
>
> *4. He brought me to the banqueting house and* ***his banner over me was love****.*

If you put Psalm 91 and these verses from Song of Solomon together, we see that when we dwell in the secret place we are under His shadow. In the Song of Solomon, they are under His shadow and brought into His house, and the banner over them is love. The secret place is the heart of God; it is the love of God. When you look at the Word and realize love is the dwelling place, it changes the way you look at Scripture.

I have found that there is a place in God when He brings us to His heart or into His love. This is a great treasure that He gives to us as His children. The Lord showed me that His greatest joy is when we come into His heart. Anna Rountree, in her book "The Heavens Opened," writes, "The Father's heart is represented by coals of fire, a flame of love. The heart of the Father is pure, a flame and holy. You must be invited to walk amid the coals of fire for although our Father loves all, not all are invited"(1999).

In order to be invited, you have to hear the knock at the door, so the Father can come in. The problem is some may not be seeking after His heart, because they do not realize it is a place they can obtain. God wants to bring us into His heart.

Let's look at what God says to Solomon and the Israelites after they build God His temple. In 2 Chronicles 7:14-16, the glory of God comes and fills the temple to the point that that priests cannot minister in it. God tells them how if there is trouble in the land such as famine, locusts or sickness, they can bring healing to the land.

> *14. If my people, which are called by name, shall humble themselves, and pray, and* ***seek my face****, and turn from their wicked ways; then will I hear from heaven and will forgive their sin, and* ***will heal their land****.*
>
> *15. Now mine* ***eyes*** *shall be open, and mine* ***ears*** *attend to the prayer that is made in this place.*
>
> *16. For now have I chosen and sanctified this house, that my name may be there forever: and mine* ***eyes*** *and* ***heart*** *shall be there* ***perpetually****.*

In this Scripture we also see the result of seeking God's face. In Deuteronomy 34:10, it says, "And there arose not a prophet since in Israel like unto Moses, whom the Lord knew face to face." If Moses could experience the face of God so can we. Some may say that God did not let Moses see His face in Exodus, but that does not mean we cannot behold His face. We cannot look at one instance in the Word and proclaim that since Moses could not see God's face at this point in his life then we cannot either. There is a progression one must go through before God will reveal His face. In Ezekiel 39:29 it says, "Neither will I hide my face any more from them: for I have poured out my Spirit upon the house of Israel, saith the Lord God." In Moses's life according to Deuteronomy, Moses came to a point where he could experience the face of God.

In 2 Chronicles 7: 15-16, we see that the result of seeking God's face is that He gives His eyes, ears and heart. When I have someone's eyes, ears, and heart, I have their face. In 1 Peter 3:12 it says;

> *For the **eyes** of the Lord are over the righteous, and his **ears** are open to their prayers: but the **face of the Lord** is against them that do evil.*

God tells them that His eyes and heart will be with them perpetually. Perpetually in this Scripture means from sunrise to sunset, it means never ending. God promises to bring us to His heart forever. The heart of God is the temple, the holy of holies, the secret place, the house of God and it is the love of God.

There is a place we can dwell with God where we will be under His shadow; it is the heart or love of God. True worship happens in the place of love, in His heart. If we look at, Jesus' example He said, " If we keep His commands we will abide in love even as He kept the Father's commands and abide in His love" (John 15:10).

> 16. *And we have known and believed the love*
> *that God hath to us, God is love; and He*
> *that dwelleth in love dwelleth in God, and God in him.*
> *I John 4:16*

According to Jesus, there is a place we can abide or stay, and it is the love of God. In John 14:2, Jesus says," He is going to prepare a place for us. In my Father's house there are many mansions." The word mansion is the same word for abode here. In John 14:3, it says:

> *And if I go and prepare a place for you,*
> *I will come again, and receive you unto*
> *myself;* ***that where I am****, there ye may be also.*

Jesus says that where He is we will be also. If He abides in love that is where He dwells. He said He abides in love. The heart of God is an actual place we can experience in the Spirit. Stop and pray now that God bring you into His heart.

As Christians we are called to love God with all our hearts, minds, souls and strength (Matthew 22:37). We are called to abide in the vine. We are told to abide in love. The question becomes how does an individual obtain this in the Spirit realm. It is through the cross that we have a right to a close relationship with God. When we know the Father and Jesus are with us we are abiding with Him. The foundation of being a true worshiper is to walk in love. This place of love brings us to the realization that the Father and Jesus are with us. It is here that true worship happens.

Chapter 2

What is Worship?

I press toward the mark for the prize of the high calling of God in Christ Jesus. Philippians 3:14

Why does a great God need praise and worship was my question to the Lord. Then in a vision one day the Lord showed me how praise and worship goes up and ministers to Him. It is a beautiful sight. It is like someone receiving a refreshing drink on a hot day, or like a cool breeze on a summer night. It is the refreshing we can give to God. The Word shows that when someone is saved the angels rejoice in heaven. So it is possible for us to cause joy to go to God and the angels in heaven. What we do on earth can cause a reaction in heaven. Jesus gave us the keys to the kingdom of binding and loosing. What we bind on earth is bound in heaven and what we loose on earth is loosed in heaven (Matthew 18:18). When we loose or release praise and worship on earth it is loosed in heaven. We can really bless the Father.

Jesus' teaching about keeping His commands shows us that as we abide in love this will in turn cause His joy to remain in us and our joy is full (John 15: 10-11). Our right response to love causes joy in heaven. David said in His presence is fullness of joy; at thy right hand there are pleasures forevermore (Psalm 16:11). Simply said God wants us to worship because He is looking for those who will love Him back. True worship is more than just singing in church. It can be part of a worship service; however it is not the end. I have been in services where we sang a few songs then sat down and waited for the service to continue. Then I have been in services where the glory comes during the worship and God takes over the service. Worship is a lifestyle where the love you have for the Father comes off you without you saying a word. There is an old saying that says if I can't say a word I will just raise my hand. The simple act of raising our hands in worship causes a reaction in heaven. The Lord told me once that as I raise my hands in a service it is a sign to Him to release power and glory. When Moses raised his arms Israel won a battle. This simple act of love of raising our hands is an example on how love will just come off of us.

Once we understand that His love is in us and that we are in His heart then what? Ephesians 3:19 says that when we know love we will come to the fullness of God. This means we come to know the Father is in us. What do we do when we come into this reality? A key to this is found in Revelation 1:6. We have all been made kings and priests.

> *And hath made us kings and priests unto God and His Father; to Him be glory and dominion forever and ever. Amen. Revelation 1:6*

As kings and priests we can give Him glory or worship. As priests to the Father we have certain duties we must do for Him. You may not have been called to a particular ministry per se, but we have all been called to be priests before Him. Remember the Lord is looking for those who will be true worshipers. A priest is to minister to God and His people. But their first ministry is to God. In Ezekiel 44:15-16, & 23, we have an example of this:

> *15. But the priests the Levites, the sons of Zadok, that kept the charge of my sanctuary when the children of Israel went astray from me, they shall come near to* ***me to minister unto me****, and they shall stand before me to offer unto me the fat*

and the blood saith the Lord God:

16. They shall enter into my sanctuary, and they come near to my table, ***to minister unto me****, and they shall keep my charge.*

23. And they shall teach my people the difference between the holy and profane, and cause them to discern between the unclean and the clean.

The Levites were the priests of God for the children of Israel. However God chose the sons of Zadok to minister to Him from among the Levites, because their heart was right before God. The Word says that many are called but few are chosen (Matthew 20:16). God calls us all to be priests before Him. Are we fulfilling our duties as priests?

We pray all the time that His kingdom come on earth as it is in heaven (Matthew 6:10). If that is the case God is to be worshipped on earth as in heaven. Daniel gives a picture of ministry before the throne of God in Daniel 7:9-10:

9. I beheld till the thrones were cast down, and the Ancient of days did sit, whose garment was white as snow, and the hair of his head like the pure wool:

> *his throne was like the fiery flame, and his wheels as burning fire.*
>
> *10. A fiery stream issued and came forth from before him:* ***thousand thousands ministered unto him****, and* ***ten thousand times ten thousand stood before him****: the judgment was set, and the books were opened.*

Here is a picture before the throne where a few ministered to God and the majority stood by the throne. It is a great privilege to stand before His throne. However, as we see in Daniel it was a special few who were allowed to minister to Him. There are many saved, many that go to church, but who are the ones who will minister to Him?

The Song of Solomon 5:1 gives a beautiful picture of those who minister to God.

> *I am come into my garden, my sister, my spouse: I have gathered my myrrh with my spice; I have eaten my honeycomb with my honey; I have drunk my wine with my milk: eat, O friends; drink, yea, drink abundantly, O beloved.*

We are as His garden that ministers to Him the fruit of the Spirit that we have by His Spirit. Jesus is the vine and we are the branches where the fruit comes off. The Father is the farmer who comes to His garden to be ministered to by us. Once He has eaten of the fruit He invites His friends to come and partake. This is where worship or ministry to the Father happens. Then His friends who He calls beloved are ministered to by the Father's presence. To be called to worship or to ministry to God is, I believe, the high calling Paul talks about in Philippians 3:12-14:

> *12. Not as though I had already attained, either were already perfect: but I follow after, if that I may apprehend that for which also I am apprehended of Christ Jesus.* ***Note:*** *(God seeketh such to worship Him, John 4:23)*
>
> *13. Brethren, I count not myself to have apprehended: but this one thing I do, forgetting those things which are behind, and reaching forth unto those things which are before,*
>
> *14. I press toward the mark for the prize of* ***the high calling of God in Christ Jesus.***

When we look at Ephesians 1:4, we see we were chosen in Christ before the foundation of the world to be holy and before Him **in love**. The sons of Zadok were chosen because they were right before God or holy. We know this because they were to teach the difference between what is holy and profane. Then they were called to come close to minister to the Father. By the cross the way was made for us, through Christ, to be holy and before the Father in love. Through the cross we have been made to worship. We see this again in Revelation 3:12,

> *12. Him that overcometh will I make a pillar in the temple of my God, and he shall go no more out: and I will write upon Him the name of my God, and the name of the city of my God, which is new Jerusalem, which cometh down out of heaven from my God: and I will write upon him my new name.*

Jesus tells the church in Philadelphia that if they overcome they will be as pillars in the temple of God. Revelation 21:22 says, "There is no temple in heaven but the Father and Jesus are the temple." So that means they will be pillars in the Father and Jesus and not go out. They are abiding in love. They are given His name which is His authority. Then it says they are given the name of the city of God which comes down out of heaven from God. He is talking about the kingdom on earth as it is in heaven. So if the people in the church of Philadelphia overcame they would abide and experience the kingdom.

Those that overcame would be holy and be before the Lord in love. They would be in the place to worship the Father on earth as He is worshipped in heaven.

The pattern of worship is to be holy and before Him in love. We see this is in the books of Ezekiel, Daniel, Ephesians and Revelation. These are the worshipers God looks for to minister or to worship Him. We have a choice: We can either be one who stands before the throne or we can be one who ministers to the Father and Jesus. The high calling is to be one who ministers to Him. The place of maturity is the place of love where we look to bless Him. We are therefore equipped to worship the Lord individually. Wherever we go can become a place of worship. Our homes, jobs, churches, and schools can become places of worship.

The question then becomes what should be our focus in our worship services? Are we just looking to experience His presence to feel good, or looking to be entertained? If this is our focus eventually someone will sing a song wrong, we will be bored, or the preacher did not preach a good enough word today. God says that He will make us joyful in the house of prayer (Isaiah 56:7). This will happen when we focus on Him and give the Father the type of praise and worship He wants and nothing will be able to keep us from experiencing His love and joy. God is calling us to maturity. 1 Corinthians 13 talks about love and how doing things without love causes our works to be as nothing. In verses 10-11, it says when I was a child I spoke as a child, but when I became a man I put away childish things when that which is perfect is come. When the Father and Jesus come we are no longer to speak or worship as a child but to do it in love. In the place of love we give Him the worship He wants. We go into the time of worship asking Him what type of worship does He want today. When His presence is manifested then we ask the Father what does He want done. What is the purpose that He wants fulfilled? This is taking worship to another level.

Chapter 3

Worship in the Spirit

...the true worshipers shall
worship the Father in spirit
and truth: for the Father seeketh
such to worship Him. John 4:23

For years I wondered what does it mean to worship the Lord in the Spirit. I studied, prayed but I did not get a true revelation of what it was for years. So don't get frustrated in your seeking the Lord, because He says if we seek Him we will find Him (Jeremiah 29:13). He also says if you lack wisdom to ask for it (James 1:5). Whenever I have had a question of the Lord He has always answered me. This is one of the exciting things I find in walking with the Lord.

As we saw in a previous chapter the pattern to worship is to be holy and before Him in love. A few years ago the Lord showed me that there is a process He takes us through which is life, glory and the kingdom. We come to life when we get saved, are water baptized and then we receive the baptism of the Spirit. Jesus says when this happens we have life for ourselves and out of our bellies will flow rivers of living water which is for the ministry of others. I want to pause here and say if you never received the Lord as your Savior ask Him to forgive you of your sins and tell Him you believe Jesus died and rose again on the third day for your sins. Once you do that you are saved, and I recommend that you find a church that will help you in your walk. Romans 10:9 says:

> *That if thou shalt confess with thy mouth the Lord Jesus, and shalt believe in thine heart that God hath raised him from the dead, thou shalt be saved.*

Now the salvation process brings us to life. Jesus said He came so we would have life and have it more abundantly. Now you can be satisfied with life or you can ask God what is next. God will then bring you to the glory of God which leads you to the kingdom of God.

The glory of God is explained to us in John 17:22-23:

> *22. And the glory which thou gavest me I have given them; that they may be one even as we are one:*

> *23. I in them, and thou in me, that they may be made perfect in one; and that the world may know that thou hast sent me, and hast loved them, as thou hast loved me.*

The glory of the God is realizing His presence in your life. In John 15, Jesus admonishes us to abide in Him as He abides in us. He says that He is the vine and we are the branches. To come into glory is to come into oneness with God. The Scripture in John 17 shows us the glory in us. In John 14:20, we see that we are in Jesus and He is in the Father. This shows that we have the same testimony that Jesus has that the Father is in me and I am in the Father. This is the glory of God. This coming into oneness causes me to realize the kingdom on earth as it is in heaven. When we have the kingdom we realize the Father and Jesus are with us here on earth. Heaven has come to us. This is the kingdom.

Jesus tells the Laodiceans in Revelation 3:21:

> *21. To him that overcometh will I grant to sit*
> *with me in my throne, even as I also overcame, and*
> *am set down with my Father in His throne.*

When we realize this for ourselves we are walking in the kingdom. Life leads to glory and glory leads to the kingdom. We must remember that we have all of this because of the cross. We have to ask God to bring us into the realization of these truths.

The question then becomes: How does this relate to worship in the Spirit? Once the Lord told me to pray that I experience the full extent of His glory. You can break the experience of the glory of God into two phases. There is the manifestation of glory in you and then there is the outward manifestation of glory.

We see the inward manifestation of glory when Paul talks about the riches of glory in Ephesians 3: 14-21. They are the following:

- *To be strengthened with might by His Spirit in the inner man. v.16*
- *That Christ may dwell in our heart by faith. v.17*

This is beyond the baptism of the Spirit, because it is a realization that Christ is in you. It is a seeing into the Spirit realm. It is as if a door within us is opened to the heavenly realm. Jesus spoke of the kingdom being within us, Luke 17:21.

21. Neither shall they say, Lo here! or,
lo there! for, behold, the kingdom
of God is within you.

This is what Paul was talking about in 1 Corinthians 13:12,

12. For now we see through a glass darkly; but then face to face: now I know in part; but then shall I know even as also I am known.

- *To be rooted and grounded in love, and to know love. v. 17&18*
  This is when you realize that God has brought you into love. He has brought us into His heart. Jesus said He keeps the Father's commands and abides in love. 2 Chronicles 7:16 shows that God will give us His heart. One of the greatest benefits of the kingdom is to know and dwell in His heart. The heart of God is the secret place talked about in Psalm 91:1. It says that they that dwell in the secret place abide under the shadow of the Almighty. In the Song of Solomon 2:3-5, it says I sat down under his shadow, and He brought me into His banqueting house, and his banner over me is love. When you put these two scriptures

together you see that the secret place is love; it is the Father's heart.

This is what Jesus was talking about in Revelation 3:20:

> 20. *Behold, I stand at the door, and knock: if any man hear my voice, and open the door, I will come in to him, and will sup with him, and he with me.*

- *To come into the fullness of God. v.19*
  The Scripture says that when I come to know love then I come into the fullness of God. In 1 Corinthians 13:12, it shows that when we come to know love we come to a place where we can behold God face to face and know Him. Jesus says when we keep His commands that He and the Father will come and make their abode with us (John 14:23). We see in Revelation 21:3 that God Himself will be with us.

> *3. Behold the tabernacle of God is with men and* ***God Himself*** *will be there...*

- *The power of God is within us. v.20*
  The same power the Father and Jesus have is in us.

- *The glory of God in the church throughout all the ages. v.21*
  This is a promise of revival for the church. We are to walk in the refreshing that comes from Jesus (Acts 3:19).

The proceeding list is the riches of glory. We experience most of these inside of us, glory in the church or revival is an outward manifestation of His glory. When we move in these riches of glory we are **living in the Spirit** or experiencing the glory or His presence inside of ourselves. Remember the Lord wants us to experience the full extent of His glory. When we move in this realm we are living in the Spirit. Paul says in Galatians 5:25:

> *25. If we live in the Spirit, let us also walk in the Spirit.*

Walking in the Spirit is the outward manifestation of the glory of God on your life. David talks about this in Psalm 139:5-10.

> *5. **Thou hast beset me behind and before,***
> ***and laid thine hand upon me**.*
>
> *6. Such knowledge is too wonderful for me;*
> *it is high, I cannot attain unto it.*

> *7. Whither shall I go from thy spirit? or whither shall I flee from thy presence?*
>
> *8. If I ascend up into heaven, thou art there: if I make my bed in hell, behold, thou art there.*
>
> *9. If I take the wings of the morning, and dwell in the uttermost parts of the sea;*
>
> *10. Even there shall thy hand lead me, and thy right hand shall hold me.*

We see the same thing in Isaiah 60:1:

> *1. Arise, shine; for thy light is come, and the glory of the Lord is risen upon thee.*
>
> *2. For behold, the darkness shall cover the earth, and gross darkness the people: but* ***the Lord shall arise upon thee****, and His glory shall be seen upon thee.*

In Psalm 91:1, those that dwell in the secret place are those who abide under the shadow of the Almighty. These are outward manifestations of the glory of God. One day in prayer the Lord said the Shekinah glory has come.

I found there is only one reference in the Bible of the Shekinah glory it is in Exodus 40:35.

> *35. And Moses was not able to enter into the tent of the congregation, because the cloud* ***abode*** *thereon, and the* ***glory of the Lord filled*** *the tabernacle.*

The word abode here is shaw-kan, and this is where the word Shekinah comes from. Here we see that the glory was on the tent and in the tent as it is for us. We also see the outward manifestation of glory in 2 Chronicles 7:1, when the glory and fire fill the temple of God. Other scriptures that show the outward manifestation of glory are:

- Exodus 34:5 – God stood with him there.
- Psalm 91:1 - ...shall abide under His shadow.
- Matthew 16:27 – The son of man shall come in the glory of His Father with His angel.
- Mark 16:20 – They preached everywhere, **the Lord working with them**. (this was after His death)
- John 14:21-23 - I will manifest myself to Him.
- John 15:5 – Without Him we can do nothing.
- Acts 10:38 - God was with Jesus.

- James 5:15 – And the prayer of faith shall save the sick, and **the Lord shall raise him up....**
- Hebrews 11:27 - By faith he forsook Egypt, not fearing the wrath of the king: for he
- endured **as seeing Him who is invisible.**
- Revelation 3:20 – I will come in and sup with him.
- Revelation 21:3 – God Himself will be with them.

There were men and women throughout the Bible who walked with God or who experienced the outward manifestation of the glory of God. The following are examples in the Word of those who walked with God or experienced the outward manifestation of glory.

- ***Israel***, *And I will walk among you, and will be your God, and ye shall be my people.* Leviticus 26:12
- **Enoch**, *walked with God,* Genesis 5:24
- **Noah**, *walked with God*, Genesis 6:9
- **Abraham**, *walk before me*, Genesis 17:1
- **Moses**, *And the Lord descended in the cloud and stood with him there*, Exodus 34:5, Numbers 12:8, Hebrews 11:27
- **Elijah**, *As the Lord lives before whom I stand*, 1 Kings 17:1
- **David**, *walk before me, as David thy father walked*, 2 Chronicles 7:17, Psalm 139:5

- **Jesus**, *yet I am not alone, because the Father is with me*, John 16:32
- **Disciples**, *And they went forth, and preached every where,* ***the Lord working with them****, and confirming the Word with signs following*, Mark 16:20

As we saw before the pattern of the true worshipers is to be holy and before the Lord in love. This is our wonderful purpose in life. These are the ones God called near to worship or minister to Him. In order to worship in the Spirit, you have to walk in the Spirit. To walk in the Spirit, Ephesians 1:4 has to become real to you in that you know that by God you are in Christ so that you will be holy and **before the Lord in love**. Being called one who walked with God was one of the highest distinctions one could receive in the Word. As I said before the high calling is to be one who worships Him. To worship Him is the high calling which is to be one who walks with Him. So to worship in the Spirit, you must walk in the Spirit, which means you are walking with God. This walk is realizing or experiencing the outward expression of His glory on a daily bases. This is what Paul talks about in Philippians 3:14:

> *14. I press toward the mark of for the prize of the high calling of God* ***in Christ Jesus.***
> ***(He is in me and I am in Him)***

The sons of Zadok did not leave the Lord which showed God love and they were to teach holiness. These were the ones called to minister to the Lord. Those that walked with Him were close to the Father and had to be holy to walk with Him. To be holy is the image of God.

Moses is an example of one who got into trouble with the religious leaders of the time, Aaron and Miriam. God said to Aaron and Miriam why were you not afraid to talk about Moses. The Lord said He speaks to the prophets in vision and dreams but Moses is not so. The Lord said He speaks to Moses plainly and face to face (Numbers 12: 1-8). According to I Corinthians 13, those that behold Him face to face are those that move in love. Exodus 34:5 says, "The cloud came and the Lord stood with him there." Moses experienced the outward glory of the Father. Moses walked with God and because of this he was able to minister or worship the Lord because of love. To walk with God means to come to the realization that you are actually walking with the Father and Jesus. If there was anyone who worshipped in the Spirit it was Jesus. Jesus, as Moses, was one who saw the Father because of love. Jesus said He kept the Father's commands and abides in love (John 15:10).

> *And the Father Himself, which hath sent me, hath borne witness of me. Ye have neither heard His voice at any time, nor* ***seen His shape****. John 5:37*

David who walked with God said one thing have I desired that I may dwell in your house all the days of my life to behold the beauty of the Lord and inquire in His temple (Psalm 27:4). To dwell in His house is to move in love and the result is to behold the Father.

> *To see your power and glory as I have seen you in the sanctuary. Psalm 63:2*

Those that walk with God can behold the Lord and it is from this relationship that worship is manifested. To be a true worshiper one requirement is that we worship in the Spirit. To worship in the Spirit you have to walk in the Spirit. Walking in the Spirit is walking with God. We are able to walk with Him because of what the Lord did at the cross. We walk with Him when we embrace the pattern of worship which is to be holy and before Him in love. This is the prize of the high calling of God in Christ Jesus. Paul said, "I apprehend that for which also I am apprehended of Christ Jesus," (Philippians 3:12). Jesus says the Father searches for those who worship Him.

We see in Psalm 14:2, the following:

> *2. The Lord looked down from heaven upon the children of men, to see if there were any that did understand and seek God.*

God is looking for you. Your high calling is to be one who worships Him in Spirit and truth. The Lord asked me one day the following question: Don't you realize the Father and Jesus are always with you? When God asks you something you have to be honest. I knew it in my head but I did not know it in my heart. I asked God to cause to me know this without any question in my mind. During the next year or so He showed me areas of unbelief and where I was perverse or my thinking was not right. First the Lord showed me that the Father and Jesus were actually within me. Then He had to show me that I was in Him and the Father. He showed me how the glory was in me and around me. I love the scripture in Revelation 21:3, God Himself shall be with them. This is what Jesus was talking about when He said believe me I am in the Father and the Father is in me (John14: 11). This is how we know Jesus walked with God. Therefore in order to worship in the Spirit we must learn to live and walk in the Spirit. As I learn to walk in the Spirit or walk with God worshipping in Spirit will come naturally to me.

Chapter 4

Worship in Truth

God is a Spirit: and they
that worship Him must worship
in Spirit and truth. John 4:24

The concept of worshipping in truth is an interesting proposition. How does one go about this? I had no clue which was not unusual for me. So I asked God for wisdom about this and He showed me the following Scripture. The way into worshipping in truth is through Jesus. Jesus says in John 14:6,

> *6. I am the way, **the truth**, and the life:*
> ***no man cometh unto the Father**,*
> *but by me.*

He goes on in that chapter and says to the disciples, "Believe me that I am in the Father, and the Father in me: or else believe me for the very works sake" (John 14: 11).

He then says, “We will do His works and greater because He will go to the Father” (John 14:12). In verse 6 He says no one can get to the Father but by Him. The truth is that it is by Him going to the Father that we can go to the Father and have the same type of relationship with the Father that He did. He is saying He is the way, the truth and the life because it is by Him that we will dwell in the Father and the Father in us. It is this truth that allows us to move in the kingdom and power. He goes on to tell them He will give another Comforter once He goes to the Father that will abide with them forever (John 14:16). In John 14: 17, He says the following:

> *17. Even the **Spirit of truth**; whom the world*
> *cannot receive, because it seeth him not,*
> *neither knoweth him: but ye know him;*
> *for He dwelleth with you, and shall be in you.*

The truth is the fact that Jesus dwells in the Father and the Father dwells in Him. In our case it is the same thing because we are in God and God is in us through the Spirit. Therefore we are in truth. In other words when we abide with the Father and Jesus we walk in truth. If we walk in truth or walk in this reality then we worship or walk in truth.

An excellent example of this is in 1 John 1: 5–9:

> *5. This is the message which we have heard of Him, and declare unto you, that God is light, and in Him is no darkness at all.*
>
> *6. If we say that we have fellowship with Him, and walk in darkness, we lie, and do not the* ***truth****:*
>
> *7. But if we* ***walk in the light****, as He is in the light, we have fellowship one with another, and the blood of Jesus Christ His Son cleanseth us from all sin.*
>
> *8. If we say we have no sin* **(when we walk in darkness-my note)**, *we deceive ourselves, and the* ***truth*** *is not in us.*
>
> *9. If we confess our sins, He is faithful and just to forgive us our sins, and to cleanse us from all unrighteousness.*

To be in truth we must abide with the Father and Jesus. How do we know if we are moving in truth? There is what I call the truth test. There are two examples we can look at in the Word. The disciples were men who were anointed with authority and power, and walked with God. Jesus is God in the flesh. Yet they found themselves in an area of unfruitfulness when they could not heal the child that threw himself in fire (Matthew 17: 15-21). When the disciples asked Jesus why couldn't they heal the child, he said it was because they were perverse and in unbelief. They were not walking in truth. After Solomon finishes the temple the manifested glory and fire of God filled the temple this was a sign that God was with them. They had the right to walk with God. Then God tells Solomon that if there is famine in the land, a time of unfruitfulness, if they were to humble themselves, pray, seek His face and turn from their wicked ways then God would hear their prayer and heal the land. In both cases in the disciples and the children of Israel they were in the place where the manifested presence of God was with them. The disciples had Jesus and the children of Israel had the temple of God. They were in a place they could walk with God. Yet in both cases if they were in a place of unfruitfulness it was because of being perverse and or being in unbelief. The answer for the disciples and the children of Israel was fasting and prayer. To be perverse or in wickedness is to be in a place of disobedience. Another definition of being perverse can also be when you have wrong thinking concerning the things of God. I found that when you sin God will forgive us, however sin is deceitful in that there are consequences to sin. It is like smoking cigarettes in the natural you do not see the damage happening on the inside of you. The Lord showed me that sin causes a veil of unbelief to come on us that the Lord has to remove from us. The Lord can be with us and we not realize it. We walk in defeat, because we are not walking in the truth. Wickedness causes God not to hear us. I was in a frustrated state once because I felt my prayer was not being answered. When the Lord answered me, all He said was I cannot hear you because of an area of disobedience. In both these previous cases God was bringing His people into a place of truth about themselves so they could walk in light which is holiness. Holiness is the difference between light and darkness. The light is holiness in this example. To walk in truth is to walk in holiness.

A person abiding with God knows that the Father and Jesus are always with you. Either you know it or you do not. You cannot fake faith. The Lord spoke to me one day and said don't you know I am with you. In those moments you have to be honest because the Lord already knows the answer. I had to admit that I did not. When the Lord showed me this He revealed to me areas where I had unbelief and moved in wickedness or perverseness. The truth test is to allow the Lord to show you what areas, if any, are causing a separation between you and God.

> *12. Take heed, brethren, lest there be in any of you* ***an evil heart of unbelief, in departing from the living God.***
>
> *13. But exhort one another daily, while it is called Today; lest any of you be hardened through the deceitfulness of sin. Hebrews 3: 12-13*
>
> *12. For the eyes of the Lord are over the righteous, and His ears are open unto their prayers:* ***but the face of the Lord is against them that do evil.*** *1 Peter 3:12*

As we have seen, the foundation to worshiping in the Spirit and truth is love. In order to move in love we must abide in Him. In order to walk in the Spirit we must walk in the glory of God or abide with Him in truth. How do we come to this glory? How do we come to the abiding place in Him? These were the questions I had for several years. I was mainly seeking for His glory, power and the kingdom. My motive for my prayer was not right many times. However, I knew that abiding in Him was the key to moving in glory, authority and power. Even though I did not have any results, I knew glory was something I could obtain. God had me in John 15 for years learning about abiding in Him. I knew that this abiding in Him would cause me to be one with Him and I thought this was how I would experience the glory of God, authority and power. My favorite Scripture during this time was Psalms 27:4:

> *One thing have I desired of the Lord, that will I seek after; that I may dwell in the house of the Lord all the days of my life, to behold the beauty of the Lord, and to inquire in His temple.*

We see in this Scripture that David sought to dwell in His house all the days of His life. I believed the result of this would cause him to behold God and to inquire or receive revelation in His temple. This Scripture gave me hope because I knew God was not a respecter of persons.

Through my study of the Word I knew that in the Old Testament the place where glory dwelled was in the tabernacle, in the Holy of Holies. In the New Testament, Jesus is the Holy of Holies and in order for Christians to find glory or His presence they need to abide in Him. All of this became the foundation in my search for the glory of God. In the beginning I was seeking after an experience and what I found was Him. The Scripture is true; He is the beginning (Alpha) and end (Omega). I sought glory and found Him. When I sought His power I found He is power. He is the end of all our seeking. I also found that every true doctrine has to have the cross as its foundation. He is the beginning. If the doctrine of glory is true then I knew the way into it had to start with Jesus.

The Lord showed me that being one with Him came before we could behold His glory. So of myself I tried to abide which I thought was praying continually. It was after much prayer, fasting, frustration, guilt, and there was even a time I gave up on receiving the glory, that I realized that I could not bring myself into an abiding relationship with God. My cry was, "God I can't do this." I even heard preachers say we can't dwell continually with God. After several years of this the Lord gave me a great revelation that changed my life. The Lord showed me (1 Corinthians 1:29-30):

> *29. That no flesh should glory in His presence.*
>
> *30.* ***But of Him are ye in Christ Jesus****, who of God is made unto us* ***wisdom****, and* ***righteousness****, and* ***sanctification****, and* ***redemption****:*

I found that by the Father we are in Christ Jesus. This changed my life forever. It is by the Father that I have an abiding relationship with Jesus. Remember to be in

Him is to have His glory and to be made perfect in one. In John 15, the Father is called the husbandman or farmer. It is the husbandman that puts the branches on the vine who is Jesus. Romans 11:16-23 talks about how we were grafted in the tree. But how does God do this? The answer is in 1 Corinthians 1:30; Jesus is made unto us wisdom, righteousness, sanctification and redemption. When we realize we have these spiritual blessings because of the cross, we will experience, walk and behold the glory of God. These blessings lead us to holiness. Holiness leads us to the presence of God. When I walk in holiness, I receive His nature and God is able to manifest Himself to me because I am holy.

Hebrews 12: 14 says:

> *Follow peace with all men, and holiness, without which no man shall see the Lord.*

In the Old Testament, the Holy of Holies was the place in the tabernacle where God met the High Priest. It was the place where the glory came. In the New Testament times the Holy of Holies is when one comes into the presence of God.

Psalms 15: 1-2 says:

> *1. Lord who shall abide in thy tabernacle?*
> *Who shall dwell in thy holy hill?*
>
> *2. He that walketh uprightly, and worketh righteousness, and speaks* ***the truth*** *in His heart.*

Jesus being made wisdom, righteousness, sanctification, and redemption leads us to holiness which leads us to God. When we talk about holiness today it has a bad connotation in some people's minds. Walking in holiness is not a bunch of do's and don'ts but it is a glorious freedom God gives us. It allows us to be like Him.

What is holiness? It is the image of God. It is the difference between light and darkness, God being the light. It is as the difference between clean and dirty water, God being the clean water.

When we look at Ephesians 1:4 and 2 Peter 3:35, we see that we have a right to holiness. Holiness is part of our destiny.

Ephesians 1: 3-4 says:

> *3. Blessed be the God and Father of our Lord Jesus Christ, who hath blessed us with **all spiritual blessings** in heavenly places in Christ:*
>
> *4. According as **He hath chosen us in Him** before the foundation of the world **that we should be holy** and without blame **before Him in love**.*

We see here that we were ***chosen to be in Him*** before the foundation of the world. We are also, to be holy and before Him in love. What a glorious destiny.

2 Peter 1: 3-4 says:

> *3. According as His divine power hath given unto us **all things that pertain unto life and godliness**, through the knowledge of Him that hath **called us to glory** and virtue.*
>
> *4. Whereby are given unto us exceeding great and precious promises: that by these ye might be partakers of the **divine nature**, having escaped the corruption that is in the world through lust.*

Peter says we have been given all things to be partakers of the divine nature. Paul in Ephesians !:3 says, "We have been given all spiritual blessings in heavenly places in Christ." If we put these scriptures together we see that we have been given all things to have the divine nature which is holiness. We see in Hebrews 12:14 and Ephesians 1:4, that with holiness we can see or know God, be in Him, in love, and be blameless.

We have been called before the foundation of the world to be holy and be in Him. We have been called to be like God. He made us in His image. Before the foundation of the world God said, "Let us make man in our own image." He did this by placing us in Christ, that we be holy and before Him in love. Holiness is the image of God. When the angels see God they cry, "Holy" (Isaiah 6:3).

Holiness is like a spiritual magnet in that once we embrace holiness it will draw us to God. The enemy has tried to lie to us to make us think holiness is drudgery. As a church if we embrace holiness and call it a good thing we will come into contact with the glory of God as never before.

The question then becomes, how do we come into holiness? The answer is in 1 Corinthians 1:30: Jesus is made unto us wisdom, righteousness, sanctification, and redemption. These are what I call the keys to intimacy with God because they all lead us to holiness.

Let's look at these keys. First of all, wisdom that comes from Jesus leads us to holiness.

Proverbs 3:35 says:

> *The **wise** inherit **glory**.*

If wisdom leads to glory, then wisdom will lead us through holiness. The way to glory is through holiness. Remember we are chosen to be in Him (which is glory), to be holy and without blame. Being in Him makes me holy. Wisdom leads me to be in Him. If I were a mathematician and made an equation I could say,

> ***Wisdom = Holiness***

The next key is righteousness. Paul exhorts us to be righteous in Romans 6:19.

Romans 6:19 says:

> *Yield your members servants to righteousness unto holiness.*

The fruit of righteousness is holiness (Romans 6:22). Therefore we can conclude that:

Righteousness = Holiness

Hebrews 10:10 and Colossians 1:22 together show us about the third key which is sanctification.

Hebrews 10:10 says:

> *By the which will we are **<u>sanctified</u>** through the offering of the **<u>body of Jesus Christ</u>** once for all.*

Colossians 1:22 says:

> *In the **<u>body of His flesh</u>** through death, to present you **<u>holy and unblamable</u>** and unreprovable in His sight.*

We see through these Scriptures that through the offering of His body we are sanctified which causes us to be holy. Therefore we can say:

Sanctification = Holiness

We can learn about our fourth key which is redemption by looking at 1 Peter 1: 16-19,

*16. … Be ye **holy**; for I am **holy**.*

*18. …ye were not **redeemed** with corruptible things,*

19. But with the precious blood of Christ,

We see God saying for us to be holy as He is holy. The Scripture goes on to say that we were redeemed by the precious blood of Jesus. So to be holy we must receive that we are redeemed. We are part of His family because of the blood of Jesus Revelation 5:9. We can therefore make the conclusion that:

Redemption = Holiness

If we break 1 Corinthians 1:30, down into a mathematical equation it would be:

Wisdom + Righteousness + Sanctification + Redemption = Holiness

We are righteous because of the sacrifice of His body and flesh on the cross (2 Corinthians 5:21). We are sanctified by the offering of His body. We are redeemed by the shedding of His blood.

John 6:56 says:

> *He that eateth my flesh, and drinketh my blood* ***dwelleth in me****, and I in Him.*

When I receive or eat and drink all that is mine because of the cross (wisdom, righteousness, sanctification and redemption), then I am holy. Because I am holy I will dwell in Him which is the glory of God, and He will dwell in me by His Holy Spirit.

Let's look at righteousness closer.

Psalms 140:13 says:

> *The* ***upright*** *shall dwell in thy presence.*

Song of Solomon 1:4 says:

> *The* ***upright*** *love thee.*

If we look at the entire chapter of Romans 8, it begins by showing us that there is no condemnation to them which are in Christ. The reason for this is because we are righteous because of the sacrifice of Jesus. Because of this sacrifice there is no place for guilt, because we are forgiven. The chapter ends asking the question: "What shall separate us from the love of God?" The conclusion that is nothing can separate us from His love. Why is this so? It is because we are righteous. Righteousness means that there is no separation between us and God.

2 Corinthians 5:21 says:

> *For He hath made Him to be*
> ***sin****; that we might be made*
> *the* ***righteousness of God in Him****.*

Righteousness means I do not have to sin. The enemy cannot make me sin. But when I receive that I am righteous it is then my choice as to whether or not I sin. I am free from sin, and the fruit of this is holiness, which is having His nature. If I have His nature then it will be natural for me to be where He is, in His presence. The rights of the righteous are:

- Healing – 1 Peter 2:24:

*Who His own self bare our sins in His own body on the tree, that we being dead to sins, should live unto **righteousness**: By whose stripes ye **were healed**.*

Because I am now righteous, I was healed at the cross. My other rights of being righteous are:

- Prosperity – Psalms 35:27:

*Let them shout for joy, and be glad, that favor my **righteous** cause: yea, be magnified, which hath pleasure in the **prosperity of His servant**.*

Psalms 112: 2-3 says:

*2. His seed shall be mighty upon the earth: the generation of the **upright** will be **blessed**.*

*3. **Wealth and riches** shall be in his **house**: and his **righteousness** endureth forever.*

Others Scriptures on prosperity are: 2 Corinthians 8:9, Psalms 37:29, Psalms 84:11.

- Reign in life and no condemnation – Romans 5:17-19, and Romans 8:1.
- The presence and love of God – Psalms 15, Psalms 17:15, Psalms 23, Song of Solomon 1:4; Psalms 140:13 says, "***The upright shall dwell in thy presence.***"

Sanctification is our next key to entering into the glory of God. Sanctification through the sacrifice of the body of Jesus has a couple of functions. When we are sanctified we are made clean.

John 17:17 says:

> **Sanctify** them through **thy truth**: Thy **word** is ***truth***.

John 15:3 says:

> *Now ye are **clean** through the **word** which I have spoken unto you.*

When we receive the Word of God, the flesh of Jesus sanctifies us and we are made clean (Hebrews 10:10).

Another function of sanctification is that it removes the consciousness of sin, (Hebrews 9:13-14). This means we are not conscious of, or thinking about sin or our shortcomings. What we become conscious of is the presence of God. We start to walk in the Spirit and not the flesh. In 2 Chronicles 7:15-16, we see that our prayers are heard because we are sanctified. In verse 15, it says God's eyes and ears are open to the prayer that comes from the temple. In our case we are the temple. In verse 16, we see the reason our prayers are heard is because God has chosen and sanctified this house. We see that sanctification also brings us to the place where we can use His name. This is the place of authority. Another blessing of sanctification happens when we combine it with our being righteous. When these two come together confidence is birthed. This is the place of answered prayer.

1 John 3:21-22 says:

> *21. Beloved if our heart condemn us not, then we have confidence toward God.*
>
> *22. And whatsoever we ask, we receive of Him, because we keep His commandments, and do those things that are pleasing in His sight.*

Our heart does not condemn us when we walk in our sanctification. In this place we also know we are pleasing to God, not because of what we do, but because of receiving the sacrifice of Jesus. However, there is a perfection process we must all go through where He will perfect our hearts. During this perfecting God does not want us to be in guilt or beat ourselves up. What we need to do is to ask for forgiveness and run back to the Father. I remember reading a book by Brother Lawrence, "Practicing the Presence of God" (1982). Brother Lawrence said he did not dwell on his failures. When he fell he went humbly to God and asked for forgiveness. He would say, "Father if you leave me to myself I will fall." We must look to the Father to keep us from falling and bring us faultless into the presence of His glory (Jude 24).

Righteousness and sanctification allow me to be confident in God. Earlier I showed how we are redeemed by the blood of Jesus, which allows us to be holy or have God's nature.

If we look deeper we see that through redemption we receive the adoption of being a Son of God. We have been grafted into the vine, who is Jesus. We are in Him; we are part of the family of God. When we receive the blood of Jesus, we become part of the bloodline of God the Father.

Galatians 4:5 says:

> *To* ***redeem*** *them that were under the law, that we might receive the adoption of sons.*

Galatians 4:7 says:

> *Wherefore thou art no more a servant, but a son: if a son, then an heir of God through Christ.*

To be an heir of God means that whatever God has is mine. I am a joint-heir with Jesus and whatever He has is mine also.

How do we come into the glory of God, the presence of God? It is by God that we are in Him, because Jesus is made unto us wisdom, righteousness, sanctification, and redemption (I Corinthians 1:30). Remember the mathematical equation:

Wisdom + Righteousness + Sanctification + Redemption = Holiness

I tried to abide and come into the presence of God of myself but I could not do it. When I realized it was by God that I was in Him this changed my life and I found myself in His presence. Paul, I believe, had the same testimony.

Philippians 3: 8-9 says:

> *8. Yea doubtless, and I count all things but loss for excellency of the knowledge of Christ Jesus my Lord: for whom I have suffered the loss of all things, and do count them but dung, that I may win Christ,*
>
> *9.* ***And be found in Him****, not having mine own* ***righteousness****, which is of the law, but that which is through* ***the faith of Christ, the righteousness*** *which is of* ***God by faith****:*

Paul, found himself in Christ once he realized he was righteous through the righteousness which is of God by faith in Christ. Once you go through this process you too will find yourself in Him. In John 6:56, Jesus said, "***He that eats my flesh and drinks my blood, dwells in me, and I in him***." When we eat or receive what His blood and flesh does for us at the cross, this enables us to dwell in Him (glory), and He is in us. This has nothing to do with what we do; this is so no flesh will glory in His presence 1 Corinthians 1:29). However, we like Paul must seek Him with our all. As we seek Him with our all eventually we will find Him. It is during the seeking process where He teaches us about His wisdom, righteousness, sanctification and redemption. This is the normal life. We can abide in Him, it is not impossible. We can dwell in His house all the days of our lives, and it is possible to behold His glory on a continual basis. This is a supernatural wonder that God wants to work in all of us. Hebrew 10:19-23, sums up how we come into the presence or glory of God. Keep in mind that glory is the manifestation of God in our lives, and we are the temple of the living God. As I abide I realize the riches of His glory in me (Ephesians 3). I also come to realize the presence of God or glory of God outside of me, the outward manifestation of glory (Isaiah 60:1-2). It is here that I walk in the Spirit or walk with God. It is here that I can walk as a true worshipper in Spirit and truth. I am able to experience these things because of the sacrifice of Jesus at the cross. The Word says as Jesus is so are we in this world (1 John 4:17). If anyone was a true worshiper in Spirit and truth Jesus was. Let's look how He worshipped in Spirit and in truth.

The lesson of 1 Corinthians 13 shows us that if we do not to move in love, our ministry is not as it should be. Jesus said, "He abided in love because He kept the Father's commands." Therefore Jesus walked with God because He waked in love. He was then able to worship in the Spirit. In 1 Corinthians 13, it also says that when I was a child I spoke as a child. This speaking can mean prayer, praise and worship. But when I became a man I put away childish things. The Lord is looking for us to have a mature worship. A worship or speech that comes from love is worship in the Spirit and truth. This is a worship that is not concerned with our needs but the needs of the Lord. We see how Jesus worshiped in the Spirit through love, but how did He worship in truth?

There are two examples that show how Jesus worshipped in truth. The first is in John 5:30 -31:

> *30. I can of mine own self do nothing: as I hear I judge: and judgment is just; because* ***I seek not mine own will,*** *but the will of the Father which hath sent me.*
>
> *31. If I bear witness of myself, my witness is not* ***true****.*

In this scripture we see that the Lord worshipped in truth by not doing His own will, but He sought the will of the Father in each situation. The result was His witness was true. He walked and worshipped in truth. The second example is in John 7: 17-18:

> *17. If any man will do His will, He shall know of the doctrine, whether it be of God, or whether I speak of myself.*
>
> *18. He that speaketh of himself seeketh his own glory: but he that* ***seeketh His glory*** *that sent him, the same is* ***true,*** *and no unrighteousness is in him.*

The other aspect of worshipping in truth is that Jesus sought to give the Father glory in whatever He did. His motive was love and to give the Father glory. It was to give the Father credit for all the great things the people were seeing. Jesus said believe me I am in the Father and the Father is in me, the words I speak I speak not of myself but the Father does the work. He was abiding, had the Word of God and God did the work (John 14:10). Jesus tells us the same thing in John 15:7. If we abide and the Word abides in us we can ask what we will and it will be done. These two scriptures are saying the same thing. This is how Jesus walked with God and worshipped in truth. John 15:7 shows we can move and walk the same way Jesus did.

I know in my life for years I had been seeking after the power of God. I would see the scriptures that said the power of God is not of ourselves. Psalm 62:11 says:

> *God hath spoken once; twice have I heard this: that power belongeth unto God.*

While I was seeking after His power, the Lord spoke to me clearly that I only wanted it for my own glory. For a time I did not understand and just asked God to clean my heart. Later what I found was that I was like Simon in Acts 8:18-19, where he offered money for the power of God. Peter told him his heart was not right. He wanted the power for his own glory. I wanted the power for my own glory in that I wanted it apart from God. What I realized later was that the Father and Jesus have all authority and power. While I am with them then I have all authority and power. I was perverse in my thinking on the power. I thought I could have it separate from God. God said I wanted it for my own glory; therefore I could not bring Him worship in truth with this type of thinking. The Word says no man will get glory in God's presence (1 Corinthians 1:29). As we abide we will realize of ourselves we can do nothing without Him.

To summarize, to worship in truth you must be holy. Holiness comes by abiding with the Father and Jesus. Abiding is knowing the Father and Jesus are with you. We have this because of the cross. When we abide we walk in truth as Jesus did. The other aspects of worshipping in truth are doing the will of God and giving the Father the glory for whatever the Father has you do. We are true when we walk in righteousness (John 7:18 & I John 1: 5-9). The Scripture says, "God only speaks righteousness, and His words shall not return, that unto me every knee shall bow, every tongue shall swear" (Isaiah 45:23). When we speak God's righteousness words then God gets the glory in what we speak, because He will do the work. This is how He gets all the glory and we move in truth (John 15: 7-8).

We can safely conclude that Jesus worshipped in Spirit and truth, and so can we because of the cross. As we see in Jesus life worship for Him was more than a song. His life was worship. This is what God is calling us to. To be true worshippers, we must abide, do the will of God and glorify the Father. We can then say that we are true worshipers of God. We will say as Paul that not as though we already attained, either were already perfect: but I follow after, if that I may apprehend that for which also I am apprehended of Christ Jesus (Philippians 3:12). We press toward the mark for the prize of the high calling of God in Christ Jesus (Philippians 3: 14). That high calling is to walk with God. When we walk with God by knowing He is there, we won't sin (I John 3:6). It is here that we can worship in Spirit and truth. It is here that we become worship, because we walk with God. When righteous men/women do rejoice, there is great glory (Proverbs 28:12).

Chapter 5

The Place of Worship

I will come in and sup with him... Revelation 3:20

When Jesus spoke about worship he said, "Worship will not happen at a particular location" (John 4:20-23). The people at that time had the mindset that they had to go to a particular location as a certain mountain to worship and find God. Some today still have that mindset that there is a certain location as a church to find and worship God. However Jesus says to the Samaritan woman that worship will not be here or there but the true worshipers will worship in Spirit and truth. The question then becomes where is this place of worship? The reason Jesus admonishes us to seek first the kingdom and His righteousness is so we will come to that place of worship He has for us (Matthew 6:33). As we have seen earlier, we can live in the Spirit which is worshipping God in the heavenly realm. Or we can walk in the Spirit where we experience God not only in the heavenly realm but we can also experience Him in the earth. This is why Jesus says, "pray thy kingdom come on earth as it is in heaven" (Matthew 6:10). The kingdom of God is realizing the Father and Jesus are with you not only in heaven but in the earth also. John 14:23 says when we love the Father and Jesus they will come and make their abode with us.

Jesus said, "Believe me I am in the Father and the Father is in me" (John 14:10). He experienced the Father in the heavenly realm and in the earth. I have found that the place of worship is wherever you are. Revelation 22:3 says," the tabernacle of God is with men and God Himself will be with them." 1 Corinthians 3:16, says, "Know ye not that you are the temple of God?"

I was reading Jeremiah 17:12, where it says "the place of my sanctuary is at my throne." This Scripture touched me and caused me to search and ask God what this means. I was reminded of the Scriptures in Revelation 21:22 and Ezekiel 43: 7.

Revelation 21: 22 says:

> *And I saw no temple therein: for the Lord God Almighty and the Lamb are the temple of it.*

Ezekiel 43:7 says:

> *And He said unto me, Son of man, the place of my throne, and the place of the soles of my feet, where I will dwell in the midst of the children of Israel forever.......*

What these Scriptures show is that when we realize the kingdom is on earth as in heaven, we come to the understanding that His throne is not just in heaven but we can experience it on earth. We have authority over the enemy because we are seated in heavenly places in Christ Jesus. When we realize the throne of God is with us on the earth we have the same authority in the earth. Jesus said, "All power is given to me in heaven and in earth" (Matthew 28:18). Since the throne is with us we must come to the realization that it is here at His throne that we worship Him. This is the place of obedience and love. This is what Hebrews 4:16, means when it says, "come boldly to the throne of grace that you may obtain mercy, and grace for your time of need."

The beautiful thing about our walk is that we can worship anywhere. The love of the Father and Jesus is always present with us because of the cross. Revelation 22:1-5 shows what a true worshiper looks like.

Revelation 22: 1-5 says:

> *1. And He showed me a pure river of water of life, clear as crystal proceeding out of the throne of God and of the Lamb.*
>
> *2. In the midst of the street of it, and on either side of the river, was there the tree of life, which bare twelve manner of fruits, and yielded her fruit every month: and the leaves of the tree were for the healing of the nation.*
>
> *3. And there shall be no more curse: but* ***the throne of God and of the Lamb shall be in it****: and His servants shall serve Him:*
>
> *4. And they shall see His face; and His name shall be in their foreheads.*
>
> *5. And there shall be no night there; and they need no candle, neither light of the sun; for the Lord God giveth them light; and they shall reign forever and ever.*

Jeremiah 17:7-13 and Daniel 7:9-11, also talks about the stream that comes from the throne of God.

Whenever you see the throne there is a river that flows from it and this is the place of power. Revelation 22:1-5, shows the benefits of being at the throne: 1) that there is no more curse there but blessing, 2) His servants will serve Him, 3) We will see His face, 4) The glory of God is there, 5) His name will be on our foreheads, and 6) We will reign forever. When we receive the kingdom the throne has come to us. If the throne is with us this is the place of His sanctuary and the place of worship. If this is the case then true worshipers are those who have received the kingdom of God in their life. They also realize that they are the temples of the living God. This is why Jesus says seek first the kingdom and His righteousness and all other things will be added to you. They realize that in order to receive the benefits of true worshipers they must worship in spirit and in truth.

Chapter 6

The Song of the True Worshiper

Give unto the Lord the glory due unto His name; worship the Lord in the beauty of holiness. Psalm 29:2

As we have seen those that worship in the Spirit are those that walk in the Spirit, or stand before God at His throne. This is the high calling of God in Christ Jesus. It is the highest designation given in the Word. In our life story to have God say that we walk with Him is special. We also looked at the three aspects of truth. We have to abide with Him, do His will and do all things for the glory of God. Our focus is on the Father. The foundation of all this is abiding in love. When we abide we know that the Father and Jesus are with us. When we abide we know that God put us in Christ that we would be holy and before Him in love. Once we find ourselves in the place of being a true worshiper, because of the cross, we can receive benefits from being at His throne as we saw in Revelation 22:5. It says we will reign forever. In this chapter will look at how the song or the worship of true worshipers helps them to reign forever. If true worship is more than singing a song, what happens when true worshippers worship or sings his or her song? What effect if any does the praise and worship have in the earth? When we do praise and worship we sing or speak to God.

In 1 Corinthians 13:11, it says:

> *When I was a child I* ***spoke*** *(worshiped) as a child, I understood as a child, I thought as but when I became a man I put away childish things.*

The thirteenth chapter of 1 Corinthians was written to show us a better way than moving in the gifts: It is moving in love. It is okay to seek after the best gifts and God honors that in our lives for a time. However, God is calling for a maturity when it comes to our giftings. For example, I can be anointed to sing worship songs but if I am not moving in love the Word says I am worshipping in part. In other words, my worship ministry is not as it should be. The Scripture goes on to say that when He that is perfect is come, or when the Father and Jesus come in glory then our ministry will be as it should. This is because they do the work. 1 Corinthians 13:12 says:

> *For now we see through a glass, darkly: but then face to face: now I know in part; but then shall I know as I am known.*

Why is beholding Him important? It is because Jesus, who is a true worshiper, said I only do what I see the Father doing (John 5:19). Doing what the Father is doing causes us to move in truth. In this place of mature worship I see how the Father and Jesus want to be ministered to and I follow them in worship.

I remember once when I was in a worship service and the praise and worship team came to a point where they moved from a praise song (fast song) to a worship song (slow song). In the natural one would think there is no problem with that, because we have done this a hundred of times in our services. It had almost become routine. It is a natural progression. On this particular day we were going into worship but I had a vision of Jesus dancing wildly. The Lord was not ready to move on. I remember being in another worship service and the Lord said He was not pleased with what was going on. The people were having a routine prayer service, yet the Lord said He was sad about how things were being run in the service. We were not doing what He wanted. We are anointed and we get into a routine, but sometimes the Lord is not pleased because we go in our own way. We tend to get lazy and not depend on the Lord for direction. It can be easy to depend on our natural abilities. The mature worshiper will be led by the Father and Jesus in worship. It is not about someone's singing ability but their position with the Lord. What happens when a true worshiper worships?

My first example is Joshua, who served Moses until he died. When Moses went before the Lord Joshua was there. When Moses died God said He would be with Joshua as He was with Moses (Joshua 1:5). So what does it mean to have God with you in a practical sense? Does having God with us in everyday life help us? Moses was so intimate with God that God descended in a cloud and stood with him (Exodus 34:5). God wants us to experience this to the point where we realize that not only is the glory/ presence of God in us, but His glory is on us. This is why Jesus says, "Believe me I am in the Father and the Father is in me" (John 14: 11). When Moses died, Joshua was in this place of the true worshiper. He is in a relational place with God where he is walking with God. God tells Joshua:

> *There shall not any man be able to stand before thee all the days of thy life: as I was with Moses,* ***so I will be with thee****: I will not fail thee, nor forsake thee.*

Joshua is now on the mission of his life. He is to lead the people into the promise land. He probably always thought Moses was going to do this job, but he is chosen. It was probably a daunting task but he was prepared by watching how Moses walked with God. Joshua had to first realize God was with him as He was with Moses. That meant God would deal with him face to face also. Everything Moses had in his walk with God, Joshua could experience also. We are joint-heirs with Jesus, so everything Jesus experienced in His walk with God, so can we. What a powerful thing!

The first obstacle Joshua had to deal with was the city of Jericho. God has Joshua get seven priests with rams' horns go before the ark and they were to go around the city seven times for seven days. On the seventh day the priests were to blow the horns and the people were to shout. When they did this the walls of the city fell down. Worship done by a true worshiper brings down the walls of the enemy. They gave God the worship He wanted then He was able to release His hand and destroy the city of their enemy.

Elisha the prophet was also a true worshiper. We know this because his and Elijah's calling card was as the Lord lives before whom I stand. He walked with God. In 2 Kings 3, the kings of Israel, Judah and Edom form an alliance to defend themselves against the Moab. The Moabites wanted to destroy Israel. The kings, while on the journey to battle, decided to check with the Lord through the prophet Elisha on whether they would be successful. 2 Kings 3: 14-15 says:

> *14. And Elisha said, As the Lord of hosts liveth, before whom I stand, surely, were it not that I regard the presence of Jehoshaphat the king of Judah, I would not look toward thee, nor see thee.*
>
> *But now bring me a minstrel. And it came to pass, when the minstrel played, that the hand of the Lord came upon him.*

Elisha the true worshiper of God says bring the minstrel, bring in praise and worship into a stressful situation. When God's people were about to be attacked by the enemy, and the leaders of the battle were looking for answers from the Lord, Elisha praises the Lord. Elisha was not even happy about being there. But as he worships, God gives him the strategy to destroy the enemy of God's people.

David was a true worshiper because God tells Solomon to walk before me as David your father walked (2 Chronicles 7:17). David, even as a young man, was known as one who was with God (1 Samuel 16:18). During this time Saul was king and he rebelled against God. God rejected Saul and opened himself to an evil spirit that troubled him. He requested that someone come and play music for him to relieve him of the trouble he felt (1 Samuel 16:18 & 23).

> *18. Then answered one of the servants, and said, Behold, I have seen a son of Jesse the Bethlehemite, that is cunning in playing, and a mighty valiant man, and a man of war, and prudent in matters, and a comely person, and* ***the Lord is with him****.*

> *23. And it came to pass, when the evil spirit from God was upon Saul, that David took a harp, and played with his hand: so Saul was refreshed, and was well, and the evil spirit departed from him.*

Here is another example of what happens when a true worshiper worships. David played and an evil spirit left Saul and he was refreshed. Praise and worship can release refreshing or revival in a place.

Jesus walked with God. In the garden He asked that this cup of death be passed from Him but then said not my will but your will be done (Matthew 26:42). In laying down His life this was the greatest form of worship and because of it Jesus was given all authority and power to destroy the works of Satan. This is why Paul says, in Romans 12:1:

> *1. I beseech you therefore, brethren, by the mercies of God, that ye present your bodies a living sacrifice, holy, acceptable unto God, which is your reasonable service.*

Paul and Silas are imprisoned for casting a spirit out of a woman. Paul walked with God yet he was beaten and thrown into jail. Paul and Silas decide to pray and sing praises in the difficult situation.

Acts 16: 25-26 says:

> *25. And at midnight Paul and Silas prayed, and sang praises unto God: and the prisoners heard them,*
>
> *26. And suddenly there was a great earthquake, so that the foundations of the prison were shaken: and immediately all the doors were opened, and every one's bands were loosed.*

As we see in the examples given, whenever a true worshiper prays, praises or worships there is a release of the power of God. The Lord showed me that when praise and worship come together, there is a release of power.

The Lord was dealing with me about how the Pentecostal movement started by William Seymour at Azusa Street, by reintroducing the baptism of the Spirit with speaking with other tongues. However, during that time the Pentecostal movement separated by race. The whites had their churches, i.e. Assembly of God churches, and the Blacks had their churches, i.e. Church of God in Christ. The Lord showed me that the white churches tended to be worship oriented. Where the Black churches were more praise oriented. The Lord said when the two come together we will see the power of God released. This is one of the reasons we don't see the power in our midst as we should because we are not worshipping in truth. God says don't bring a sacrifice to me when someone has an ought against you without you fixing it (Matthew 5: 23-24). In order, for revival to be in our churches we must deal with racial issues on both sides.

The next question we must ask is why is it that when a true worshiper worships is the power of God is released? David answers that question in Psalm 29:1-11:

1. *Give unto the Lord, O ye mighty, give unto the Lord glory and strength.*
2. ***Give unto the Lord the glory due unto His name; worship the Lord in the beauty of holiness.***
3. *The voice of the Lord is upon the waters: the God of glory thundereth: the Lord is upon many waters.*
4. *The voice of the Lord is powerful; the voice of the Lord is full of majesty.*
5. *The voice of the Lord breaketh the cedars; yea, the Lord breaketh the cedars of Lebanon.*
6. *He maketh them also to skip like a calf: Lebanon and Siron like a young unicorn.*
7. *The voice of the Lord divided the flames of fire.*
8. *The voice of the Lord shaketh the wilderness: the lord shaketh the wilderness of Kadesh.*
9. *The voice of the Lord maketh the hinds to calve, (causes birth), and discovereth the forests: and in His temple doth every one speak of His glory.*
10. *The Lord sitteth upon the flood: yea. The Lord sitteth King forever.*

11. *The Lord will give strength unto His people; the Lord will bless His people with peace.*

Worshiping in the beauty of holiness is abiding in Christ. Christ is made unto us wisdom, righteousness, sanctification, and redemption (I Corinthians 1:30). These make us holy. At the foundation of the world we were placed in Christ so we can be holy, without blame before Him in love (Ephesians 1:4). It is here at the throne that God releases His voice and answers our prayers with power. This is the place of true worship in Christ, before the Father in love. This is the high calling of God in Christ Jesus, Philippians 3:12-14 says:

> *12. Not as though I had already attained, either were already perfect: but I follow after, if that I may apprehend that for which also I am apprehended of Christ Jesus.*
>
> *13. Brethren, I count not myself to have apprehended: but this one thing I do, forgetting those things which are behind, and reaching forth unto those things which are before.*
>
> *14. I press toward the mark of the high calling of God in Christ Jesus.*

The thing we have been apprehended for is to be a true worshiper by walking with God. John 4:23 says, “God seeketh such to worship Him.” Because of the cross we all have the opportunity to be true worshipers to sing His song so the power of God can be released in whatever situation we find ourselves.

When we worship the voice the Word of God is released. When we worship, praise, fast or pray we touch the heart of God and He releases His voice or Word for a situation. It is here that faith is birthed, because faith works by love (Galatians 5:6).

During praise and worship many times we feel the presence of God coming into a service and we stop. What we should be doing is asking God, what is His purpose in coming in our midst. It is during these times that we have found the Lord will release His Words. The Words may be for salvation, healings, deliverance, refreshing or prosperity. Every service can be different and exciting. In His presence is fullness of joy and at His right hand are pleasures forevermore (Psalm 16:11).

The Lord promises to make us joyful in His house of prayer (Isaiah 56:7). His garment of praise causes the spirit of heaviness to leave (Isaiah 61:3).

Chapter 7

Faith birthed by Worship

Faith works by love, Galatians 5:6

As we saw in the last chapter there are certain things we do as believers that release the voice of God. Prayers, fasting, giving, worship and praise done with the right attitude touches God's heart and He releases His voice. The release of His voice causes faith to be birthed in us and then we can pray as we ought. The true worshiper is one who knows how to get their prayer answered before the throne of God. This is another outgrowth of being before the Lord and reigning forever. An example of this would be Elijah. We established earlier that he walked with God and was a true worshiper. Elijah's testimony was "as the Lord lives before whom I stand." James goes onto describe Elijah as a man as we are. Think about it: Elijah was just like you. What would you look like if you knew that whenever you prayed God would answer? The way you look at yourself would completely change.

James goes onto describe Elijah as a righteous man. We see in James 5:16-17:

> *16. .....the effectual fervent prayer of a righteous man avails much.*
>
> *17. .....Elijah prayed and it did not rain for 3 years and six months.*

The true worshiper is righteous and a fervent effectual prayer warrior. The true worshiper knows how to get his or her prayer answered. The book of Matthew is our guidebook from Jesus on how to get our prayers answered. The following is the progression Jesus takes us through:

- Matthew 6:9-10 – v.9. After this manner therefore pray ye: Our Father which art in heaven, hallowed be thy name. v. 10. Thy kingdom come, Thy will be done in earth, as it is in heaven.

We are to start our prayer with worship. Father how great is your name. I have found that as we seek the Lord He will show us His different names. I remember the Lord said to me that He is I Am. He is my Deliverer, Healer, Abundance, Provision, Mighty God, Miracle Working

God, Able, Power, God of Fire, God of Love and the Lord of Hosts. The Lord showed me that He is so powerful that just speaking His name will release power. This is called having faith in His name (Acts3:16).

Exodus 34:5 says:

> *5. The Lord descended in the cloud and stood there proclaiming His name.*

Many times God will show us His name so we will have confidence that He can move in our situation. Nothing is impossible with God. When we know His name we know that if He is healing or provision then we know it is ours in heaven because that is what God is for us in our particular situation. Since we are heirs of God then what He is in heaven belongs to us because we are His children. Hallowed be thy name Lord. When we worship His name we are saying to God we believe His is able to move in our situation.

The other aspect of saying our Father was very controversial in Jesus day. The disciples said, "Jesus show us how to pray (Luke 11:1)." The first thing He tells them to say is Our Father. This was controversial because when Jesus healed a man on the Sabbath the religious leaders were mad because in their eyes Jesus broke the law. They would have probably let this go, however when He said my Father they wanted to kill Him. They said He was making Himself equal to God. The disciples knew this and when they ask Jesus to teach them to pray He tells them to say Our Father. This is the very thing that would get them killed. To receive the kingdom we must realize that God is our Father. The Lord once told me the kingdom is about family where we are heirs of God and joint-heirs with Jesus Christ. This is why we must receive the kingdom as a little child. To receive the kingdom we must see God as our Father. What a powerful concept, that the God of heaven is our Father.

The next part of the prayer is, thy kingdom come, thy will be done on earth, as it is in heaven. After worshiping His name the five words as it is in heaven are the most powerful part of this prayer. We are asking for what belongs to us in heaven be released to us in the earth. The question becomes how do we bring what is mine in heaven to the earth? How do we bring my healing, prosperity etc. to the earth? How do we bring the manifestation of the throne of God on earth? Ezekiel 43:7 says:

> *7. And He said unto me, Son of man, the place of my throne, and the place of the soles of my*

feet, where I dwell in the midst of the children of Isreal for ever......

Jesus and Paul say that the kingdom is in us. However, when we ask for the kingdom to come on the earth we are asking for the outward manifestation of the kingdom on the earth. Not only is the kingdom in us but it surrounds us. This is the difference of living versus walking in the Spirit. Hebrews 11:27 says, "that Moses withstood the king as seeing Him who is invisible". You come to know the Father and Jesus are always there.

- Matthew 6:33 – But seek first the kingdom of God and His righteousness and all these things will be added to you.

Jesus is telling His followers not to worry about what you will eat, drink or wear. He said the Father knows we have need of these things but seek first the kingdom and these things will be added to you.

Matthew 6 ends with Jesus saying seek first the kingdom and starts off chapter 6 showing the disciples to pray for the kingdom first.

The question then becomes what is the kingdom? The main scripture that shows us what the kingdom is in Hebrews 12: 22-28.

> *22. But ye are come unto mount Zion, and unto the city of* ***the living God****, the heavenly Jerusalem, and to an innumerable company of angels.*
>
> *23. To the general assembly and church of the firstborn, which are written in heaven, and to* ***God the Judge of all,*** *and to the spirits of just men made perfect,*
>
> *24. And to* ***Jesus the mediator of the new covenant****, and to the blood of sprinkling, that speaketh better things than that of Abel.*
>
> *25. See that ye refuse not Him that speaketh. For if they escaped not who refused that spake on earth, much more shall not we escape, if we turn away from Him that speaketh from heaven:*
>
> *26. Whose voice then shook the earth: but now He hath promised, saying, Yet once more I shake not the earth only, but also heaven.*

27. And this word, Yet once more, signifieth the removing of of those things that are shaken, as of things that are made, that those things which cannot be shaken may remain.

*28. **Wherefore we receiving a kingdom which cannot be moved**, let us have grace whereby we may serve God acceptably with reverence and godly fear:*

When we receive the kingdom we are receiving the Living God, God the Judge of all, and Jesus the mediator of the new covenant. They are the healing, provision and everything we need that is in heaven. When we receive the kingdom we realize we are seated with Him in heavenly places (Ephesian 2:6). Isaiah 9:6, talking about Jesus says the government/kingdom shall be on His shoulder. He is the kingdom.

I had been seeking God about what is the kingdom. One day He tells me it is about family. I did not understand it at the time. Then He showed me Mark 10: 13-15:

13. And when they brought young children to Him, that He should touch them: and His disciples rebuked those that brought them.

14. But when Jesus saw it, He was much displease, and said unto them, suffer the little children to come unto me, and forbid them not: for of such is the ***kingdom of God****.*

15. Verily I say unto you, Whosoever shall not receive the kingdom of God as a little child, he shall not enter therein.

To receive the kingdom we must come into a revelation that God is our Father. When Jesus is asked by the disciples how to pray, the first thing He teaches them is to say is, "Our Father which art in heaven," (Matthew 6:9). This was very controversial in Jesus' time because in John 5: 17-18, we see that the Jews were ready to kill Jesus because by calling God Father He made Himself equal with God. Then Jesus tells His disciples to say our Father. They must have been thinking that Jesus is trying to get us killed. Then Jesus says, "Do not worry about what you eat or drink but seek first the kingdom and His righteousness and all these things will be added to you," (Matthew 6:32-33). Jesus says seek first the kingdom and in the Our Father prayer that is the first thing He prays that the kingdom come. He says Father how great is your name. The various names of God show what He can do. The name I AM embodies all that God is. Then when we pray thy kingdom come we are asking that all God is come to us. We are praying that His kingdom of heaven come on the earth. If I ask a king for his kingdom I am asking for his land, economy, people, military and everything that pertains to the government. What we are asking for is that we experience heaven on earth. People say all the time when people die that there will be no sickness in heaven. Well if the kingdom of heaven is on earth then there should be no sickness on the earth. Realizing the kingdom in your life is essential to our worship. Remember Jesus says to seek the kingdom first. When we do this we come to the place of His throne to worship him. The Word also shows that the kingdom is within us (Luke 17:21). Romans 14:17 says,

> *17. For the Kingdom of God is not meat and drink; but righteousness peace, and joy in the Holy Ghost.*

Jesus is righteousness (1 Corinthians 1:30). He is the prince of peace (Isaiah 9:6). He is also our joy, for in His presence is fullness of joy (Psalm 16:11). Experiencing the kingdom within us is living in the Spirit. When we pray thy kingdom come on the earth as it is in heaven we are asking to experience the kingdom in the earth. This is walking in the Spirit. You know by faith that Jesus is not only in you, but He is with you in the earth realm. Daniel 7:27 says, “We as saints will experience the kingdom under heaven." We will not just experience the kingdom in the heavenlies but we will experience His tangible presence in the earth. They that dwell in the secret place of the Almighty will abide under His shadow (Psalm 91:1). Thou hast beset me before and behind (Psalm 139:5). The Lord descended in the cloud and the Lord stood with Moses there (Exodus 34:5). The Lord wants to stand and to walk with us now. Revelation 21:3 says, "The temple of God is with man and **God Himself** will be there." When I come into this revelation then I am walking with God. I am partaking in the kingdom on the earth. This is heaven on earth. What a wonderful experience we have as His children. True worshipers are those who realize God is their Father. This is the foundation of being a true worshiper. A true worshiper is one consumed with the love of God. The love of God is in them and it surrounds them.

We must receive the kingdom as a little child by receiving God as our loving Father. Redemption by the blood of Jesus makes us part of the family of God. Revelation 5:9-10 says:

> *9. And they sung a new song, saying, Thou art worthy to take the book, and to open the seals thereof: for thou wast slain, and hast* ***redeemed us*** *to God by thy blood, out of every kindred and tongue, and people, and nation;*

10. And hast made us unto our God kings and priests: and we shall reign on the earth.

The Father and Jesus are with me. They are the kingdom. Isaiah 9: 6 -7 says of Jesus,

6. For unto us a child is born, unto us a son is given: and the ***government shall be upon His shoulder****: and His name shall be called Wonderful, Counselor, The mighty God, The everlasting Father, The Prince of Peace.*

7. Of the increase of ***His government*** *and peace there shall be no end, upon* ***the throne of David****, and upon* ***His kingdom****, to order it, and to establish it with judgment and with justice from henceforth even forever. The zeal of the Lord will perform this.*

The government or kingdom is on the Lord's shoulder. Jesus is the kingdom. So when I say thy kingdom come I am saying Lord come and handle my situation. I preached a sermon once titled, who is in your boat? When the disciples were going through the storm and Jesus was asleep they awaken Him saying don't you care if we perish. Jesus answered why are you fearful and in unbelief?

He was telling them don't you realize the Son of God is with you. Don't you realize nothing is impossible for me? The kingdom consists of salvation, healing, deliverance, prosperity etc.

When Jesus comes He embodies all of that. When Jesus stepped in Peter's boat after a night of fishing and nothing was caught, Jesus tells them to put the net on the other side and it was filled with fish (John 21:6). When Jesus is in your boat even your business will prosper. Who is in your boat? The Lord will teach you areas where you have fear, unbelief or are perverse in the way you are thinking so that your prayers will be answered. The opposite of these is faith. The following scriptures are a key for us understanding faith, which is important in our prayers being answered.

- Matthew 16: 15-18- v. 15. He saith unto them, But whom say ye that I am? v. 16. And Simon Peter answered and said, Thou art the Christ, the Son of the living God. v. 17. And Jesus answered and said unto him, blessed art thou, Simon Bar-jona: for flesh and blood hath not revealed it unto thee, but my Father which is in heaven. v. 18 And I say unto thee, that thou art Peter and upon this rock I will build my church; and the gates of hell will not prevail.

In this passage Jesus is talking to the disciples about faith. As we walk with God and minister to Him through praise and worship, we are loving Him back. When we minister to Him, He will minister back to us many times through releasing His voice by speaking His Word to us. The Word causes faith to be birthed. The Lord showed me that some have moved in the realm of power but did not go beyond that realm. The realm beyond power is love. Love and power together are a powerful force. This is the place of creative miracles. This is why obedience is critical because without it love and power cannot come together as they should. Love and power go together, which are attached to obedience to cause the Word to create what we pray. It is like a scientific diagram of an atom. If you have triangle obedience would be at the top, love on one side and power on the other. The Word of God would fill the middle. If the Word comes to us and obedience or love is missing then our prayer cannot be answered as it should be. We see this in I Corinthians 13, where if we have faith to move mountains and do not have love the ministry will not be as it should be. You may get results but God will not be glorified. Moses hit the rock in Number 20:11-12, when he was supposed to speak to it. The water came and the people were ministered to but God was upset and was not glorified in that situation.

In this place of love when we receive His Word it causes faith to be birthed in us. Faith comes by hearing and hearing by the Word of God (Romans 10:17). Faith is the true worshiper's main weapon, because through it authority and power are released. If God was a gun, faith would be the trigger and the bullet would be the Word.

We have seen that praise and worship is important because God is looking for someone who will love Him back. In this place of love, praise and worship cause a reaction in God where He releases His voice and faith is birthed. When we praise and worship God in hard situations, we are telling God that He can handle the situation. Coming to Him in faith causes our faith to grow. There comes an agreement between God and us.

Jesus said the baptism of the Spirit will be as rivers coming out of our bellies (John 7:38). Psalm 29:3 says, "The voice of the Lord is upon the waters." God speaks His Word and it comes forth from us by His Spirit. Ephesians 3:20 says:

> *20. Now unto Him that is able to do exceeding abundantly above all we ask or think, according to the power that works in us.*

Jesus said, "The words that I speak to you I speak not of myself: but the Father that dwells in me, He does the works," (John 14:10). Isaiah 55:11 shows what happens when His Word is released.

> *11. So shall my Word be that goeth forth out of my mouth: it shall not return unto me void, but it shall accomplish that which I please, and it shall prosper in the thing whereto I sent it.*

Praise and worship in love causes faith to work. So how does faith work for the true worshiper? It is a critical element in the true worshiper's walk.

I remember years ago I asked God what is faith and how does it work. All He said to me at the time was that faith is a substance. I said Lord no disrespect but can you give me a little more? Years later I found that the answer He gave me could not have been more correct and simple. The main scriptures on faith are in Hebrews 11:1 and 11:6. They say:

> *1. Now faith is the substance of things hoped for,*
> *the evidence of things not seen.*

6. But without faith it is impossible to please Him: for he that cometh to God must believe that He is, and that He is a rewarder of them that diligently seek Him.

To explain these scriptures we need to look again at Matthew 16:13-19:

13. *When Jesus came into the coasts of Caesarea Philippi, He asked His disciples, saying, Whom do men say that I the Son of man am?*

14. And they said, Some say that, thou art John the Baptist: some, Elijah; and others, Jeremiah, or one of the prophets.

15. He saith unto them, But whom say ye that I am?

16. And Simon Peter answered and said, Thou art the Christ, the Son of the living God.

17. And Jesus answered and said unto him, Blessed art thou, Simon Bar-jona: for flesh and blood hath not revealed it unto thee, but my Father which is in heaven.

18. And I say also unto thee, That thou art Peter, and upon this **rock** *I will build my church; and the gates of hell shall not prevail against it.*

What was Jesus saying here to Peter? He was saying that upon this rock I will build my church. Many have interpreted this Scripture in many ways. Some say Jesus was saying that Peter is the rock. However, if you put this Scripture with Hebrews 11:1, you will look at it in a different way.

I believe Jesus was saying upon this rock or faith will I build my church. Jesus is faith, therefore He is the rock (1 Corinthians 10:4). Jesus told Peter that the revelation he received was from God. When we receive a Word from God it produces faith. Hebrews 11: 1, says, "Faith is a substance of things hoped for and evidence of things not seen." What are we hoping for? I Timothy 1:1 says,

> *Paul, an apostle of Jesus Christ by the commandment of God our Savior, and* ***Lord Jesus Christ, which is our hope.***

In Hebrews 11:6, it says, "We must believe God is and is a rewarder of them that diligently seek Him." I used to think that if I hoped for something and diligently sought God for it He would give it to me. My faith focus was on the things I wanted and not on Christ. Faith believes that He is or exists. If I diligently seek Him, as the scripture says, I will find Him. My faith focus needs to be on

Christ. The evidence of things not seen is the Word of God that comes from the Father, which produces faith. I have evidence of things not seen because the Father has shown me the unseen. Faith comes by, or is produced by hearing the Word of God. When we hear about Jesus and our spirit is quickened or made alive we have faith to believe Jesus is real and we get saved. We have evidence of things not seen.

Faith believes He is or is with you. This is what Peter was saying when he said thou are the Christ the Son of the living God. Jesus calls this faith, this Word, the rock He will build His church on. Hebrews 12:2 says, "Jesus is the author and finisher of faith." Jesus is faith; He is the rock the church is built on.

Ephesians 2:20 says:

> *20. And are built upon the foundation of the apostles and prophets, Jesus Christ Himself being the* ***chief corner stone****.*

The Father and Jesus are faith. They are the substance or rock of things hoped for and the evidence of things not seen. The following Scriptures show how the Father and Jesus are the rock:

> *God is **my rock**, He is my **shield**. 2 Samuel 22:3, note: Ephesians 6:16, talks about the shield of faith.*
>
> *Who is God, save the Lord? and who is a **rock** save our God? 2 Samuel 22:32*
>
> *The **Rock** of Israel. 2 Samuel 23:3*
>
> *The **rock** of my salvation. Psalm 89:26*
>
> *....upon this **rock** I will build my church. Matthew 16:18*
>
> *Jesus the chief corning **stone**. Ephesians 2:20*
>
> *The **shield** of faith. Ephesians 6:16 (He is my shield 2 Samuel 22:3)*

Why is it important for the true worshiper to know about faith? Faith says that the Father and Jesus are with us. It is important for individuals to know that even their faith comes from God. This is so no one can glory in His presence. Part of worshiping in truth is to bring glory to God. Jesus was always pleased when people came to Him in faith. The focus of their faith was that He could help them. It was that He had the power to set them free. The focus of their faith was on God.

When Jesus was talking to the disciples at coasts of Caesarea Philippi, I heard Minister Perry Stone preach on how this was where idol worship occurred. In this place was a body of water that came up from the rock that was called the gates of hell. It was in this setting that Jesus prophesied to the demons in that place that the rock that the church will be built on will destroy the gates of hell. He was telling hell He would be raised by the power of God. He was telling hell that this faith, the rock can be used as offensive and defensive weapons.

In Matthew 16:19 it says:

> *And I will give unto thee the keys of the kingdom of heaven:*
> *and whatsoever thou shalt bind on earth shall be bound in heaven:*
> *and whatsoever thou shalt loose on earth shall be loosed in heaven.*

Faith is an offensive weapon when we can bind and loose the works of the enemy. The Lord showed me that the binding and loosing is initiated in heaven. The Father and Jesus initiate or do the work in the heavenlies. Then we are to speak what they say in the earth and have the answer to prayer. This is why the Word says Jesus is the author and finisher of our faith (Hebrews 12:2).

The enemy tries to block our prayers as he did with Daniel. He tries to put barriers around our mind, body, soul and spirit. The true worshiper realizes that his or her victory is in praise and worship. God said He inhabits the praises of His people. That means He is right there. Praise and worship reinforces our faith, in that it causes us to realize that the Father and Jesus are right there to answer our prayer. Faith works by love (Galatians 5:6). We are to use this Rock to smash the gates of hell, the barriers of the enemy. Jesus gives us the formula to prayer in Matthew 17:20 it says:

> *20. And Jesus said unto them, Because of your unbelief: for verily I say unto you, If ye have faith as a grain of mustard seed, ye shall say unto this mountain, Remove hence to yonder place: and it shall remove: and nothing shall be impossible unto you.*

What Jesus was saying was that if we just know a little bit that God is with us, then we have faith as a grain of mustard seed and we can speak to the mountains in our lives and they will be removed. The Lord spoke to me one day and said don't you know that the Father and I are always with you? I knew it in my head, but it was not real in my heart. The Lord then showed me where I had unbelief. When we sin God forgives us because of the blood of Jesus, however, sin can cause a veil of unbelief to come on us and we not even realize it. This is why God told the children of Israel not to forget Him in the land of promise.

Being perverse can also hinder your prayers. The disciples walked with Jesus yet he called them perverse. They were not doing sinful things because they were with Jesus. They were walking with God and yet had issues. This is a good lesson for us because we are always going to be perfected by love. You can be perverse in that your thinking can be off. The Lord showed me for example that I wanted the power of God for my own glory. He showed me Simon in Acts 8:15-23, where he tried to purchase the power of God. Peter told him that his heart was not right. It is the same motive of Satan wanting more power than God. Satan said, "I will ascend my throne above God's." The Lord said He could not answer me because of this it was not because He did not love me. God must get the glory. The Lord said that when He spoke about the mountains being removed He remembered Psalm 97:3-5:

> *3. A fire goeth before Him, and burneth up His enemies round about.*

4. His lightnings enlightened the world: the earth saw, and trembled.

5. ***The hills melted like wax at the presence of the Lord****, at the presence of the Lord of the whole earth.*

How does God answer prayer in the Bible? He answered by fire. John the Baptist said, "Jesus would be baptized with the Holy Ghost and fire." The baptism of fire is the baptism of power.

Acts 10:38 says, "Jesus was anointed with the Holy Ghost and with power/fire." The following scriptures show how God answers by fire.

- Daniel 7:10- A fiery stream issued and came forth from Him.
- Psalm 50:3 - Our God shall come and not keep silence, a fire shall devour before Him.
- Psalm 97:3-5 - A fire goes before Him and burns up His enemies round about.
- Isaiah 30:33 - ... the breath of the Lord like a stream of brimstone doth kindle it.
- Isaiah 33:14 - Who will dwell in the devouring fire?
- Isaiah 66:15 - ...for behold the Lord will come with fire.

The hills melt as wax because the Lord is with you and He is fire. He is the substance or rock of things hoped for and the evidence of things not seen. In the heavenlies He speaks and it is done.

We receive what He says and pray in faith. This is how we believe we receive when we pray, because we hear from heaven. When we pray in faith then the Lord does the work and burns your mountain up. If there was ever a true worshiper it was Jesus. He uses this principle of prayer in John 14:10:

> *10. Believest thou not that I am in the Father in me? The words that I speak unto you I speak not of myself: but the Father that dwelleth in me, He doeth the works.*

We see in Ephesians 6:16, faith is also a defensive weapon.

> *16. Above all, taking the shield of faith, wherewith ye shall be able to quench all the fiery darts of the wicked.*

To be in a place of praise and worship when you are going through adversity tells God that you believe He is able to work the situation out. Fear, despair and discouragement cannot stay on you when you walk in a place of praise and worship. This worship is faith that stops the attacks of the enemy from being successful. It is a shield of stone. Psalm 16: 11 says:

> *11. Thou wilt show me the path of life: in thy presence is fullness of joy; at thy right hand there are pleasures forevermore.*

In His presence is fullness of joy. You're in a place of faith because you know He is there and it is a place of joy. This joy is produced by an attitude of praise and worship which causes Him to be glorified. We see this again in Isaiah 61:3:

> *To appoint unto them that mourn in Zion, to give unto them beauty for ashes, the oil of joy for mourning, the garment of praise for the spirit of heaviness; that they might be called the trees of righteousness, the planting of the Lord, that* ***He might be glorified***.

The shield of faith quenches the fiery darts of the enemy in the place of praise and worship (Ephesians 6:16). When David played for Saul the tormenting spirits that plagued his mind had to leave.

As we have seen the place of worship is a place of love. This love opens the door to His life, glory and kingdom. In the place of love we have everything we need because the Father and Jesus are present with us. The place of love is the kingdom of God. The Scripture says come boldly before the throne of God (Hebrews 4:16). The Lord showed me that if we are already at the throne we do not have to come boldly. It is the same way with the kingdom. Jesus in Matthew 6:33 says, "Seek first the kingdom and His righteousness and all things will be added to you." He starts off the chapter by teaching us to pray: Our Father hallowed be thy name, thy kingdom come thy will be done on earth as it is in heaven. He is showing us in the beginning of the chapter how to pray for the kingdom and then the chapter ends saying seek the kingdom. It is the same kingdom. If we seek something, God says we will find it. If we seek the kingdom we will find it. When we receive the kingdom we do not have to pray thy kingdom come because the kingdom is with us. If the kingdom is with us then the Father and Jesus are with us, and we are in the place of answered prayer.

There are two types of prayer at the throne that will get us results. The first is praying in tongues. The Word says that praying in tongues builds our faith and keeps us in the love of God (Jude 20-21). The Spirit is also making intercession for us according to the will of God (Romans 8:26-27). This type of prayer goes directly to God's heart at the throne and brings Him glory. The Holy Spirit is called the Spirit of Truth (John 14:17). This is why praying in the Spirit is the purest form of prayer because the Spirit of Truth is praying through us according to the will of God. Those that do His will are those that worship in truth (John 5:30-31). We are in truth not because of our own righteousness but because of Jesus.

The other type of prayer is the prayer of faith. The following Scriptures will give us insight into the meaning of the prayer of faith:

James 5:15 says:

> *And **the prayer of faith** shall save the sick, and **the Lord shall raise him up**, and if he has committed sins, they shall be forgiven him.*

Acts 3:16 says:

> *And His name through **faith in His name** hath made this man strong, whom ye see and know: yea, the faith which is by Him hath given him this perfect soundness in the presence of you all.*

Acts 4:10 says:

> *Be it known unto you all, and to all the people of Israel, that by* ***the name Jesus Christ of Nazareth****, whom ye crucified, whom God raised from the dead,* ***even by Him*** *doth this man stand here before you whole.*

In Acts 3 Peter and John pray for the healing of a lame man. When the people try the give praise to them Peter tells them it is through faith in His name that made this man strong. In Acts 4:10, he says, “that praying in His name causes Jesus to come and do the healing”. Peter says, “even by Him.” Then in James 5:15 it says, “The prayer of faith shall save the sick, and the Lord shall raise him up.” The similarity between both verses is that the Lord will raise them up. So the prayer of faith is to pray in the name of Jesus. In John 14-16, Jesus says six times that if we ask anything in His name He will do it.

John 14: 13 says:

> *13. And whatsoever ye shall ask in my name, that will I do, that the Father may be glorified in the Son.*

When we pray in Jesus name He will answer us so the Father is glorified. This is another way we worship in truth, because they that worship in truth look to glorify the Father. The Lord showed me that when we pray in His name it is as a key that opens the door to the power of God.

Philippians 2:9-10 says:

> *9. Wherefore God also hath highly exalted Him, and given Him a name which is above every name:*
>
> *10. That at the name of Jesus every knee should bow, of things in heaven, and things in earth, and things under earth;*
>
> *11. And that every tongue should confess that Jesus is Lord, to the glory of God the Father.*

The true worshiper, who prays the prayer of faith, prays in the name of Jesus at the throne.

This prayer releases the authority and power that comes from the Father and Jesus and by this we will reign forever and ever (Revelation 22:5).

This is a benefit of being a true worshiper. James 5:16 says, "The effectual fervent prayer of the righteous availeth much." This is because faith has been birthed in us through worship, and God has released His voice.

Chapter 8

Beholding His Face

...but then face to face, I Corinthians 13:12

There is a visual dimension that we can experience as a true worshiper. It is another benefit in walking with God and being before His throne (Revelation 22:4). It is a place of intimacy. Throughout the Bible we are admonished to seek the Lord's face. We see that Moses was known as one who was face to face with God. We see where Isaiah, Ezekiel, Daniel, David, Solomon, Jesus, Peter, Mark, John and Paul all experienced seeing the face of God. In 2 Chronicles 7:14, God says, "If you humble yourselves, pray**, seek my face** and turn from your wicked ways then I will hear from heaven." God goes onto say that not only will He give His ear but He will also give His eyes and heart. 1 Peter 3:12, says, "God's eyes are on the righteous and His ears are attentive to their prayers." When you have someone's eyes and ears you have their face. We see this again in 1 Corinthians 13:12:

> *For now we see through a glass, darkly; but then* ***face to face****: now I know in part; but then shall I know even as also I am known.*

We know that Paul is talking about the glory of God here because in 2 Corinthians 3:18, he says:

> *But we all, with open face beholding as in a glass the glory of the Lord, are changed into the same image from glory to glory, even as by the Spirit of the Lord.*

Jesus says in John 17:24:

> ***Father I will that they also****, whom thou hast given me, be with me where I am; that they may* ***behold my glory****, which thou hast given me: for thou lovedst me before the foundation of the world.*

David says in Psalm 27:4:

> *One thing have I desired of the Lord, that will I seek after; that I may dwell*

> *in the house of the Lord all the days*
> *of my life,* ***to behold the beauty of the Lord,***
> *and to inquire in His temple.*

David says in Psalm 63:2:

> *To see thy power and thy glory, so as I have*
> ***seen thee*** *in the sanctuary.*

Hebrews 11:27:

> *By faith He forsook Egypt, not fearing*
> *the wrath of the king: for He endured,*
> ***as seeing Him who is invisible.***

We see from these Scriptures that it is for us to behold the Lord. It has been my experience that there are several ways the Lord will manifest Himself to us visually. There are outward visions of glory the Lord can give us as Peter and the disciples had on the mount of Transfiguration.

There is the vision of seeing Him in the Spirit. Paul says it correctly where he says at first it is as looking in a mirror darkly. The Lord told me once that this is something that we must practice. This is the vision of those who are living in the Spirit. Then there is the vision of those that behold Him that walk in the Spirit. It is not seeing Him outwardly as in an open vision but it is as it says in Hebrew 11:27, where Moses saw Him who is invisible. It is seeing Him in the natural world in the Spirit but it is different than the seeing of those living in the Spirit or seeing Him within. It is seeing Jesus in the natural realm.

Psalm 91:1 says:

> *He that dwelleth in the secret place*
> *of the most High shall abide* ***under***
> ***shadow of the Almighty****.*

Exodus 34: 5 says:

> *And the Lord descended in the*
> *cloud, and* ***stood with him there****,*
> *and proclaimed the name of the Lord.*

Why is this important for the true worshiper? It is important because God wants all His children to be face to face with Him. Paul shows that as we are face to face we will know Him as we are known and we will be changed into the same image. The image of God is holiness. In Hebrews we see that Moses overcame adversity by seeing

Him who is invisible. Beholding Him builds up our faith. It is a wonderful blessing to not only hear Him but we can also see Him on a continual bases.

Acts 2: 17 says:

> *And it shall come to pass in the last days, saith God, I will pour out of my Spirit upon all* flesh*: and your sons and your daughters shall prophesy, and* ***your young men shall see visions****, and your old men shall dream dreams*:

David's testimony was in Acts 2:25:

> *For David speaketh concerning him, I* ***foresaw the Lord always before my face****, for he is on my right hand, that I should not be moved:*

Jesus testimony was in John 5:37:

> *And the Father Himself, which hath sent me, hath borne witness of me, Ye have neither heard His voice at any time, nor* ***seen His shape****.*

Why is beholding the God important for the true worshiper? If we look at Jesus' example He said in John 5:19:

> *Then answered Jesus and said unto*
> *you, The Son can do nothing of Himself,*
> *but what* ***He seeth the Father do****: for what*
> *things soever He doeth, these also doeth*
> *the Son likewise.*

There is a level of ministry where we are to not only hear how the Lord wants to move in a situation but we see how He wants to move. There are times in prayer ministry where I can see the Lord moving in a particular way. The only thing I do is to say I see God moving or doing a certain thing. After that it is the Lord that completes the work. We were in worship service one time and the praise and worship team went from praise songs to more worshipful songs. However, I saw the Lord fervently dancing and He wanted us to continue what He was doing. It is important to give the Lord the type of worship He wants. This is so the Lord can release in our services what He wants.

In the Old Testament prophets were called seers because they saw in the Spirit realm. Habakkuk 2:1 says:

> *I will stand upon my watch, and set me upon the tower, and will* ***watch to see*** *what He will say unto me, and what I shall answer when I am reproved.*

Here is an instance where the prophet spoke what he saw happening. It is giving a now word. You are not speaking of something that will happen in the future but you are speaking a fresh word from God. Jesus said, "The Words I speak to you I speak not of myself but the Father that is in me is doing the works," (John 14:10).

Jesus tells the disciples to watch and pray. We are to see what is going on in the Spirit and pray accordingly. This type of prayer will change our services and ministries, and God is glorified.

Our testimony can be that we behold the face of the Lord daily. The reason why people have not experienced this is because they did not realize what seeking His face is all about. Jesus said in John 17:24 that it is His will that we behold His glory. The question is why are we waiting? We all should seek His face as true worshipers. In Revelation 22:1-5 it says the Lord is on His throne and His people will serve Him. There is no curse there and they will see His face. We can experience this now.

Chapter 9

Who are you at the table?

I will come in and sup with him... Revelation 3:20

The true worshiper as we have seen is one who fully participates in the kingdom of God before His throne. They have received the kingdom as little children because they see God as their Father. The true worshiper is one who walks in the Spirit. They are those that walk with God. The true worshiper is one who worships in truth in that they look to glorify God. They are those who walk in love and power. Obedience is the factor that brings the love and power together in their lives. The true worshiper's main ministry is to worship God by coming before His throne. As we saw in Daniel 7:10, there are many that stand before His throne. There are a lot fewer that worship at His throne. The true worshiper is one who worships at His throne.

In Revelation 3:20, Jesus is talking to church folks saying, "I stand at the door and knock. They that open the door will I come to and eat with them." God is looking for those who will fellowship with Him. It is out of this fellowship that will lead us to sitting in His throne with Him in a place of authority.

In John 12:1-9, tells of a dinner that Jesus was invited to after Lazarus is raised from the dead.

John 12:1-9 says:

1. *Then Jesus six days before the Passover came to Bethany, where Lazarus was, which had been dead whom He raised from the dead.*
2. *There they made Him a supper; and Martha served: but Lazarus was one of them that sat at the table with Him.*
3. *Then took Mary a pound of ointment of spikenard, very costly, and anointed the feet of Jesus, and wiped His feet with her hair: and the house was filled with the odor of the ointment.*
4. *Then saith on of His disciples, Judas Iscariot, Simon's son, which should betray Him,*
5. *Why was not his ointment sold for three hundred pence, and given to the poor?*

6. *This he said, not that he cared for the poor; but because he was a thief, and had the bag, and bare what was put therein.*
7. *Then said Jesus, Let her alone: against the day of my burying hath she kept this.*
8. *For the poor always ye have with you; but me ye have not always.*
9. *Much of the Jews therefore know He was there: and they came not for Jesus' sake only, but that they might see Larzarus also, whom He had raised from the dead.*

There are also accounts of this story in Matthew 26:6-13, Mark 14:3-9, and Luke 7:36. When you look at all the scriptures you see the following about the key players at this dinner:

- **Simon the leper** - His house was in Bethany and he invited Jesus to come eat at his house. He was a Pharisee, one of the religious leaders of the day. He was also the father of Judas Iscariot, the disciple that would betray Jesus.
- **Mary** - The woman who came with the alabaster box of ointment. She was the sister of Lazarus and Martha. In Luke 7:36 she is known as a woman in

the city who was a sinner. It does not say Mary but it does say this event happened in Simon's house.

- **Lazarus** - a friend of Jesus who Jesus raised from the dead.
- **Martha** - served the dinner. In Luke 10:38, she was mad at Mary for not helping her serve.
- **The disciples** - Jesus followers
- **Pharisee's and chief priests**
- **Many Jewish people who came to see Lazarus**

Jesus is invited to a dinner party. There are many people there for different purposes and motives. Simon the host is known as a leper and Pharisee. The Bible does not say it but I wonder if Jesus healed him of his leprosy. The bible says Simon did not greet Jesus as was customary for their culture. He may have been worried about what his fellow Pharisee church leaders would say.

The Pharisees are at the table, proud of their position and wisdom trying to find a way to discredit and kill Jesus. They were even ready to kill Lazarus because Jesus and the disciples were shaking up the religious system. This was a religious system that validated their existence, and Jesus was turning the Jews to Himself.

Lazarus was there at the table. Think of what was going through his mind as Jesus sat at the table. Here is a man who was raised from the dead. The Bible says many Jews were saved because of his testimony. I would have liked to have heard Lazarus tell his testimony. What did he see in heaven?

Martha was there probably serving Jesus with joy because of Jesus being there. He was the man that raised her brother from the dead.

The disciples, still in the throes of their faith development, did not always know what to think.

Then there were the people who came to see Lazarus. The Bible says they did not come for Jesus' sake only.

Then Mary comes in, the woman with a box of oil and anoints Him and cleans His feet with her tears and her hair. This was an expensive box of oil. She was a woman who did not have a good reputation and was known as a sinner. She sees her brother healed and has an opportunity to be at dinner with Jesus. In front of the leaders of the church, the followers of Jesus and people in the town who knew of her reputation she makes a bold move and ministers to Jesus. Jesus said it was to prepare Him for His burial; she must have received revelation from God to do what she did. Jesus told her and Martha at Lazarus' tomb "if you believe you would see the glory of God" (John 11:40). When Isaiah saw the glory all he could say was "I am unclean" (Isaiah 6:5). She falls at Jesus feet realizing she is wretched and yet not condemned because of love. Remember Mary, Martha and Lazarus were siblings. However at some point she realized the divinity of Jesus.

People were mad at her sacrifice of love and intimacy with Jesus but it is what He wanted. She fulfilled her purpose when she was in the presence of God. The only other person looking to minister to Jesus was Martha. Martha ministered in a way that was familiar to her. The question is would she have been open to minister to Jesus in another way if God lead her to do that? When praise and worship come together power is released. But the other people were not in unity in the worship that was being offered to Jesus. They were too busy being judgmental and angry.

Judas was mad because Mary wasted the expensive oil on Jesus, and said the money could have been used on the poor. Here is an example of doing something good without love, and in Jesus sight it was as nothing. The chief priests wanted to kill Jesus and Lazarus. Simon was being rebuked in love because he did not treat Jesus correctly as a host. Judas was also Simon's son. So Judas did not even treat Jesus as he should have in his father's house. This was pretty much a dinner where Jesus was not welcomed by a majority of the people there. Many invited to sit with Jesus yet only two ministered to Him, Martha and Mary. It was like the vision in Daniel 7 where only a few ministered to God. Psalm 23:5 is a prophetic picture of Jesus in this story. It says:

> 5. Thou preparest a table before me in the presence of
> of mine enemies: thou anointest my head with oil;
> my cup runneth over.

Mary through her worship fulfilled this prophetic word. This is why it is important to be obedient in worship because many times we will not know what we are accomplishing in the Spirit.

If this dinner party was your church or home who would you be in this scenario? Would you be a true worshiper that worships Jesus even though it is not popular? The religious leaders said if Jesus was a prophet He should have known what type of woman Mary was. Mary was persecuted because of love. Sometimes the cost of being a true worshiper is you will not be understood and persecuted because of doing the right thing. This was her fellowship of suffering, to be rejected by her community, church leaders and family and yet there was room for her at the table with Jesus. He considered what she did true worship.

Jesus wept over Jerusalem because they did not realize their time of visitation. We as church folks can be those who miss the visitation of Jesus just like those that were at the dinner at Lazarus house. Some at the dinner party were distracted and missed the significance of being in the presence of Jesus.

God is still looking for true worshipers. Jesus said what Mary did will always be remembered. She was remembered for her worship. What a great legacy to have, to be remembered for your worship. It is my prayer that we all have this great legacy, and be remembered in heaven and earth for our worship.

God bless,
Rick Rannie

References

Lawrence, B. (1982). The practice of the presence of God. Pennsylvania: Whitaker House.

Rountree, A. (1999). The heavens opened. Florida: Charisma House.

Scripture quotations from the King James Version of the Bible.

Pastor Rick Rannie is available for ministry at your church, or conferences. He can be contacted at the following address:

634 Southgate Dr
State College PA 16801

Telephone - 814 404 3065
Email – rick.rannie@ucjc.org